New Zealand on a Budget

by Linda Linse
and
Gary Cheledinas

 An Odyssey Publication

An Odyssey Publication

Printed by:
Shields Bag and Printing Co.
Yakima, Washington U.S.A.

Library of Congress Catalog Number 79-89442

ISBN 0-934494-00-2

Printed in the United States of America

The photo on the front cover is of the Punakaiki Rocks (Pancake Rocks) on the South Island. On the back cover — Aratiatia Rapids near Taupo.

*For Tom Lockyer,
one of New Zealand's
"unofficial ambassadors."
We appreciated your hospitality
and enjoyed your company.
Thanks.*

*And a special thanks to
Tim Davis
for the terrific drawings.*

*We'd also like to express our appreciation
for the help we received from the local
Public Relations Offices and Government
Tourist Offices throughout New Zealand,
and for all the suggestions and advice from
the people at Air New Zealand.*

CONTENTS

PART THREE — THE SOUTH ISLAND IN DETAIL

MAPS

ILLUSTRATIONS

INTRODUCTION

People asked us why we went to New Zealand, after all, it's not like saying you're going to Europe or the Orient! But the answer we gave was always the same — for such a small country, the land is so diverse. It has everything — mountains, glaciers, beaches, rolling hills, farms, and cities, but mostly it's the people.

The Kiwis are friendly and warm, and they're so helpful that they make traveling in New Zealand carefree and fun. About 3 million people are scattered all over the North and South Islands, and the majority are honest and share a passion for traveling. They say that's why they love to help travelers — and to share experiences and find out more about the world that sometimes seems so far away. During your stay, make an effort to meet the people — you'll be glad you did and chances are that they will be, too!

Inflation is attacking the world and New Zealand is getting its share. So if you find that some of the prices we've listed have been raised, please forgive us — we have included the most up to date figures we could get. In any event, you'll find that New Zealand is a really good choice for a vacation on a budget — prices are low and quality is high.

One other favor. With all travel guides, updating is the key. If you have any suggestions for the next edition, please write and let us know. Odyssey Publishing Company, Route 3 Box 698, Yakima, Washington 98901 U.S.A. Thanks!

Part One

NEW ZEALAND
North Island
WHANGAREI
AUCKLAND
HAMILTON
ROTORUA
TAUPO
GISBORNE
NEW PLYMOUTH
TONGARIRO
NAPIER
WANGANUI
PALMERSTON NORTH
South Island
NELSON
PICTON
WELLINGTON
KAIKOURA
GREYMOUTH
FRANZ JOSEF
FOX GLACIER
CHRISTCHURCH
MOUNT COOK
WANAKA
MILFORD SOUND
QUEENSTOWN
TE ANAU
DUNEDIN
INVERCARGILL
Stewart Island

A HISTORICAL LOOK

According to Maori legend, that magical Polynesian Maui fished the North Island up out of the sea with a special hook. The South Island was the canoe he fished from — Stewart Island was the anchor-stone.

Then in the middle of the tenth century, another Polynesian, Kupe, discovered New Zealand while chasing a giant octopus. After spending some time in the uninhabited place and naming it Aotearoa, which means Land of the Long White Cloud, he went back to his homeland, Hawaiki, with instructions about how to return.

By the 1300s things had gotten bad in Hawaiki. There just wasn't enough food available in the overpopulated islands. When plans were being made by some of the Maoris to leave, they recalled Kupe's accounts of Aotearoa, fertile and empty of people. The Maoris that left Hawaiki made up the Great Migration.

When they arrived, however, there were people living in Aotearoa already — two other canoes had made the journey in the 12th century. Today these original settlers are called the Moa Hunters because they hunted the moa, a huge (up to 10 ft. tall) flightless bird. They were so successful, in fact, that moas are now extinct.

The Maoris lived happily in their new land for about 300 years. They had abundant food, including birds, fish, paua (abalone), and kumaras (sweet potatoes) that they grew from seed they brought from Hawaiki. They carved, wove, tattooed their bodies, and one of their favorite pastimes was making war on the neighboring tribes, then following the fighting with ritualistic cannibal feasts.

The first clash between Maori and pakeha (white man) was in December of 1642, when Abel Tasman discovered New Zealand. His ships, the Heemskerck and the Zeehaen, sailed into Golden Bay, on the northern coast of the South Island. Tasman was on a mission for the Dutch East India Company looking for new trade centers, so when he saw smoke he stopped to check it out.

War canoes greeted the ships, only coming close enough for the Maoris to shout threats. The next day, as a cockboat went from one ship to the other carrying a message, war canoes intercepted it and killed four men.

Tasman quickly left the area and headed north. He never landed, however, because he found no friendly natives and no safe harbors. He named the islands Staten Landt, mistakenly thinking that they were connected and formed the west coast of a huge southern continent whose east coast was South America. The continent idea was proved wrong, and the country was eventually named Nieuw Zeeland, Zeeland meaning "sea land." The spelling was anglicized after the British claimed the country.

On October 9, 1768, Capt. James Cook dropped anchor near present-day Gisborne. His Tahitian interpreter was able to communicate with the Maoris, so he was able to avoid Tasman's fate. During his six-month circumnavigation of the islands he became friendly with the natives and traded with them. He named many of the landmarks and waterways of the country and charted most of the coastline during his stay. Cook's very favorable comments about New Zealand and its people paved the way for subsequent colonization efforts.

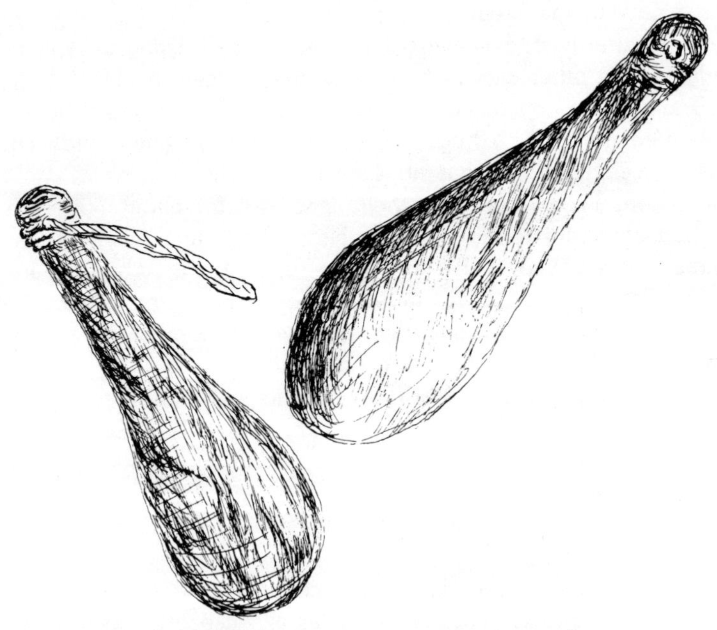

Meres are Maori weapons made from greenstone or stone.

The first Europeans to arrive were sealers, in the 1790s. By 1820 they had nearly destroyed the once-abundant seal population and the sealing industry came to a halt. The whalers had arrived around the turn of the century, however, to begin their exploitation. The flurry of activity only lasted 35 years or so — by 1840 customs duties were trimming profits, besides, the whales were nearly gone, too.

The traders started coming early in the 19th century. They traded muskets and rum to the Maoris for flax and kauri wood. The kauri forests were nearly destroyed by greed, too — today only two major stands remain, one at Waipoua in Northland, the other in the Coromandel Ranges.

Preserved heads brought a high price for a time, and the Maoris increased their warfare practices so they would have more heads to trade for more muskets to make more war . . . After a chief spotted some of his friends and relatives among a trader's inventory he appealed to a missionary, who talked to the governor of New South Wales, and the exportation of preserved heads was declared illegal.

To put it literally, many of those first Europeans weren't the cream of the crop. Their ranks included ex-convicts and men who signed onto ships with no questions asked. There were no qualms about killing Maoris, stealing food, even stealing women. And the Maoris' numbers were falling rapidly. They had no resistance to the pakehas' diseases — typhoid, smallpox, and influenza killed thousands.

The first missionary to arrive in the wayward land was Samuel Marsden. He landed in the Bay of Islands, and preached his first sermon on Christmas Day of 1814, at Oihi. At first the missionaries had few converts — many Maoris felt that Christianity wasn't right for warriors. But as the Maori population fell, they became afraid of their whole race dying, and at times the pakeha God seemed more powerful than all of their gods.

The missionaries opened schools, and used Maori translations of the Holy Bible as textbooks. They taught the Maoris to grow European crops so they weren't as dependent on the kumara for life. Tribal warfare was curbed when the Maoris accepted the pakeha "God of Peace."

But it wasn't all roses. The puritanical code of the missionaries caused most of the pre-European Maori art to be destroyed (much of the work was sexually symbolic). Tattooing was banned. And with the undermining of the authority of the ancient gods, the chiefs lost much of their prestige. Tribal society as it had been began to deteriorate.

Things went from bad to worse. Thievery, kidnapping, and prostitution were rampant. But the Crown didn't have the time or money to get involved with the tiny land. There were big problems in North America, the West Indies, and South Africa occupying all the available resources. In 1831, after the French began to show interest in New Zealand, King William sent James Busby to be British Resident. Poor Busby, however, was ineffectual, as he had no power to enforce any laws.

Then the New Zealand Company began to send settlers and the Crown sent Capt. William Hobson, who gathered some of the most powerful Maori chiefs at Busby's residence. The purpose of the meeting was to sign a treaty declaring British sovereignty. On February 6, 1840, 45 chiefs signed the Treaty of Waitangi (Busby's home, now called Treaty House, was at Waitangi, Bay of Islands). Five hundred more chiefs from all over the country later added their signatures.

Unfortunately, the Treaty signalled the beginning of problems between Maori and pakeha. The settlers needed land, and the Maoris often didn't want to sell. Although the Maori rebels were fewer in number (only about 5000) they had been practising war for hundreds of years and were very good at it. In fact, to make it "more fair" they sometimes allowed the British to sneak away for food or ammunition! Reinforcements, both men and guns, finally affected their toll on the Maoris. After twenty years of fighting the Land Wars, the battle ended in mutual respect.

New Zealand became self-governing in 1852, and received Dominion status in 1907. Many call it the "original welfare state" because of laws passed near the turn of the century on workmen's compensation, minimum wages, child welfare, and old age pensions — things that were unheard of elsewhere in the world at that time.

World War I saw a country wrapped up in its patriotism and duty to the rest of the world. Although the total population was only one million, 100,000 Kiwis went to the war! She proved herself a power in her own right.

SOME MAORI CULTURE

Maoris make up about ten percent of the country's population. The best place to learn about their culture is in Rotorua, but we'll give you a short introduction here.

Carving, both in wood (especially totara, which is fairly soft, yet durable) and greenstone has long been a maori art. Many pieces served both utilitarian and artistic uses. The carving has changed since pre-European times, with very few pre-European artifacts remaining.

Two of the larger types of carved items are the whare runanga (meeting house) and the traditional war canoe. Meeting houses can be seen all over the North Island and good examples of canoes are the one at Waitangi (near Treaty House) and another at the War Memorial Museum in Auckland. The Auckland museum, in fact, has an especially good collection of Maoritanga.

Pre-European Maori music consisted of chants, songs of lament (waiata tangi) and songs of love (waiata aroha). They were sung almost in a monotone, usually ranging only over three or four notes. Musical instruments were made of stone, wood, and bone, and because they had no drums, foot-stomping and chest and thigh slapping served for rhythm. Today's Maori songs are said to be based on harmonies from early hymnals.

Dancing ranges from the ferocious haka (war dance) to the gentle and rhythmic poi dance, performed only by women.

Weapons were made of wood, bone, stone, and greenstone. There were four main types of weapon: the patu (short club), the taraha (a weapon of hard wood about 5 feet long), the te whatewha (an axe-like long weapon), and the mere (a flat greenstone or stone club).

Tattooing used to be very common among the Maoris. It was a sign of status — men often had tattoos covering their faces, buttocks, and thighs. Women of high rank were tattooed on the lips and chin. The process was painful — a chisel with a serrated edge was tapped with a mallet, then soot was rubbed into the wound to provide color.

The Maori alphabet consists of only 15 letters — the vowels a, e, i, o, and u, and the consonants h, k, m, n, ng, p, r, t, w, and wh.

Here's a simple pronunciation guide for the vowel sounds:

> a sounds like the short a in "gather"
> e sounds like the short e in "pen"
> i sounds like the long e in "clean"
> o sounds like the long o in "go"
> u sounds like the oo sound in "broom"

Each vowel is pronounced and there are no dipthongs in Maori. Wh is voiced as "f" and ng is pronounced as in ringing. Emphasis is nearly always on the first syllable.

Here is a list of some Maori words you might see, and their translations:

ahi — fire	manu — bird
ao — cloud	maunga — mountain
ata — shadow	mere — flat club
atua — spirit or god	moana — sea
awa — river	motu — island
haka — dance	pa — fortified village
hangi — earthen underground oven	pakeha — white person, European
ika — fish	puke — hill
kai — food	rangi — sky
kumara — sweet potato	roto — lake
mana — prestige	tapu — forbidden, sacred
tea — white or clear	waka — canoe
tiki — human image	whanga — bay or inlet
wai — water	whare — house

A Maori warrior depicted during a "haka" or war dance, offering a challenge.

BACKGROUND INFORMATION FOR THE TRAVELER

Now that you've decided to go to New Zealand there's obviously some red tape required. To start with, almost everyone needs a passport (except Aussies, and British or Irish citizens who have been granted permanent residence in Aussieland). For visits up to six months, the following don't even need visas — U.K. citizens, Canadians, Irish, and many Western Europeans. Visitors from West Germany, Iceland, Finland, and Malta can stay up to three months without a visa. And if you're from the U.S., Japan, Tahiti, or New Caledonia, you can stay up to 30 days without a visa.

If you want to stay longer than the allotted "free time," you must apply for a visa. To do that, write to the nearest New Zealand Government Tourist Office:

330 Collins Street
Melbourne, Victoria
Australia

288 Edward Street
Brisbane, Queensland
Australia

115 Pitt Street
Sydney, N.S.W.
Australia

Suite 530
630 Fifth Avenue
New York, NY 10020

Suite 970
Alcoa Building
One Maritime Plaza
San Francisco, CA 94111

Suite 1530
Tishman Building
10960 Wilshire Blvd.
Los Angeles, CA 90024

Rathenauplatz 1a
Frankfurt, West Germany

New Zealand House
Haymarket
London S.W. 1Y 4TQ England

New Zealand's monetary system is dollars and cents, although occasionally you'll get a coin that's left over from the shilling and pence days. Denominations of coins are 1^c, 2^c, 5^c, 10^c, 20^c, and 50^c, with each getting larger along with its value. The currency you'll most commonly see are $1, $2, $5, $10, and $20 bills — and again, the larger the bill, the more it's worth. Travelers checks are exchanged at a higher rate than foreign notes, so as well as being safer, they're actually worth more. The money market changes rapidly, but at press time these exchange rates were in effect:

$1 Australian	buys $1.13 New Zealand
$1 Canadian	buys $ .83 New Zealand
£1 British	buys $2.14 New Zealand
$1 United States	buys $ .95 New Zealand

Most visitors fly to New Zealand, and unless you're coming from Australia or one of the nearby Pacific islands it'll take a long time! Fares are going down more all the time, but to get the cheaper ones you usually have to book way ahead and pay in advance — so plan to see your travel agent early to avoid buying an expensive ticket! Because New Zealand is so far away from Europe and North America, many travelers make a few stops on the way, and often it doesn't cost much more. If Singapore, Fiji, Pago Pago, Hong Kong, or Hawaii sound like fun — check it out.

HOW'S THE WEATHER?

New Zealand has a four season climate, but to those of us from the Northern Hemisphere it's upside down. Summer is from December to February, warm, but not generally **hot** in most parts of the country. Expect highs in the 70s and 80s (about 20° to 30° C). Fall starts in March and by June it's winter. Winter in New Zealand means a coat, but lots of areas throughout the country rarely see snow. September marks the beginning of spring.

Rain is spread throughout the year — there isn't really a "rainy season" except on the West Coast of the South Island where it rains nearly all the time (over 200 inches annually!). The northern areas of both islands are the places to find sunshine — one of the reasons that Nelson and the Bay of Islands are such popular spots. The east coasts also get less rain than their western counterparts.

An acquaintance from Auckland told us, "If you don't like the weather, wait a minute," and that proved to be true during our stay. The weather can change drastically within a few hours — a beautiful morning can become a wet afternoon, and vice versa.

When packing for your trip remember one thing — your collapsible umbrella may become your best friend!

Centigrade	Fahrenheit
− 15	5
− 5	23
0	32
5	41
10	50
20	68
25	77
30	86
40	104

TRANSPORTATION

Air travel is obviously the most expensive way to get from point A to point B, and New Zealand is no exception. If you get pressed for time, however, it might be a necessary expense. Air New Zealand and Mount Cook Airlines both travel inter-city, and scenic flights are available all over the country at the tourist spots.

The government-owned rail network travels only between the main cities (as far as passengers are concerned) but it's really comfortable to travel by train and the cost is about the same as taking the bus. If you plan to see the country quickly, there is a Railways Tourist Pass that costs $90. It allows unlimited train, bus, and ferry travel on the Railways network for 14 consecutive days and would be a good deal if you're pressed for time.

Railways Road Services (government-owned), Newman's Coach Lines, and Mount Cook Landlines comprise the bulk of the bus system. Between these major companies almost all areas of the country have bus service. The buses of all three lines are comfortable and usually stop every two hours or so for food and conveniences. All sorts of people ride the bus — your fellow passengers are usually quite pleasant.

All sorts of rental vehicles are available, from automobiles to small motor homes (motor caravans). Avis and Hertz are big in car rentals — their prices are usually higher, too. A small car with unlimited mileage runs about $30 per day, plus gas (which is expensive) and insurance ($3 a day, $15 a week). There are smaller rental agencies in the larger cities whose prices are much more economical. The only problem is that you usually have to return the car to the same place that you picked it up from. One company in Auckland, for example, North Harbour Rental Car Co., has Chevy Chevettes for about $55 a week and 9^c a km.

To drive in New Zealand you'll need an international driver's license or a valid Australian, Canadian, U.S., British, South African, West German, or Fijian license (or a New Zealand one, of course!). If you're from North America be prepared to drive "backwards" until you get used to driving on the left-hand side of the road! It's confusing. (And

Air Routes and Fares

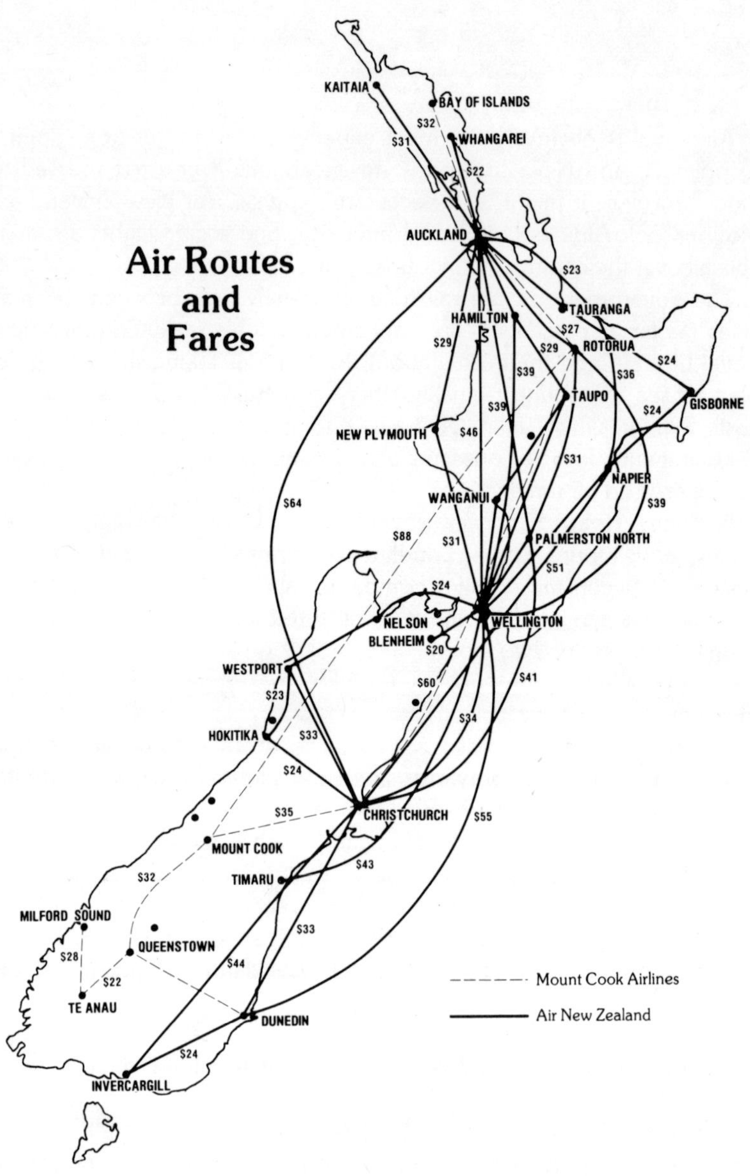

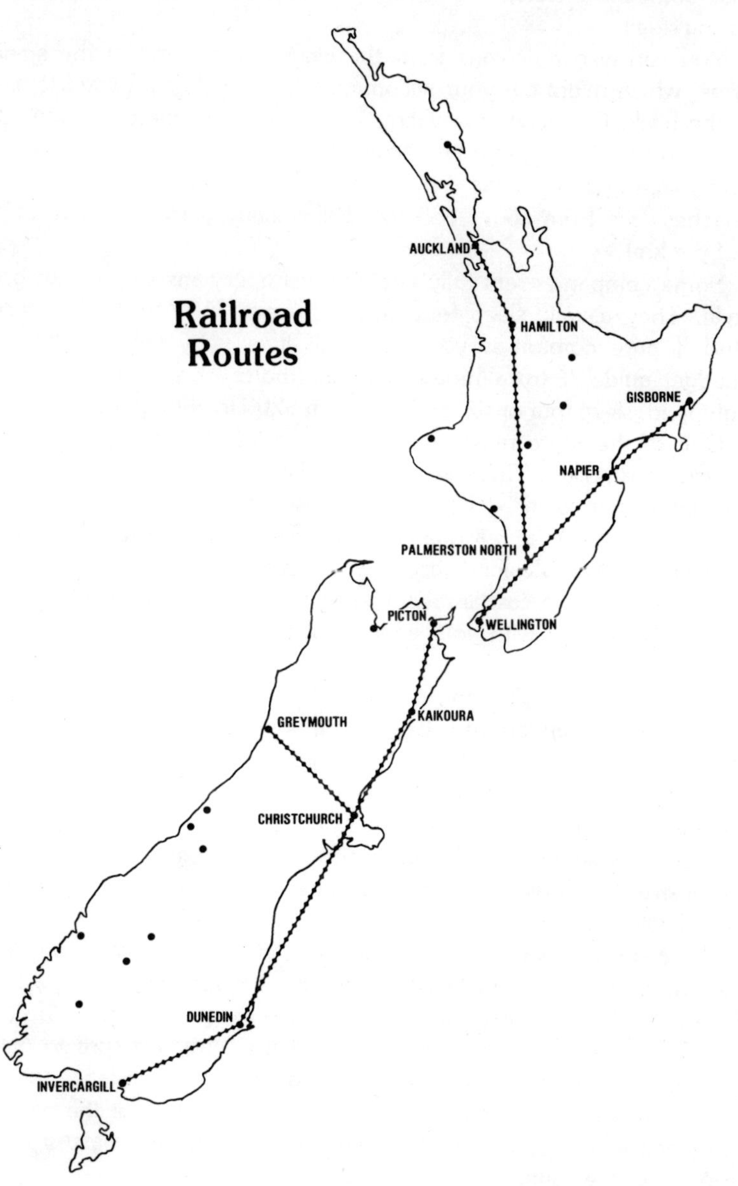

Railroad
Routes
AUCKLAND
HAMILTON
GISBORNE
NAPIER
PALMERSTON NORTH
PICTON
WELLINGTON
GREYMOUTH
KAIKOURA
CHRISTCHURCH
DUNEDIN
INVERCARGILL

you'll feel really stupid when you walk to the car, get in, and realize that someone's stolen the steering wheel — you're sitting on the wrong side!)

You can also rent vans from the biggies and some of the smaller firms, which might cut your accommodation bill if you'd want to sleep in the back. Or if you're traveling with a group — there are vans that have up to 12 seats, and by dividing the costs by 12 it should become pretty reasonable. Vans run about $85 to $120 a week, "mini coaches" are from about $85 to $135 weekly (all prices plus 11ᶜ or 12ᶜ per km).

Some companies rent fully equipped camper vans so you can go in style. They usually sleep four and cost from $180 to $250 a week. And if pure comfort is your game (if it is, why did you buy this "budget guide"?) try a motor caravan (motor home). They are fully equipped, sleep four or six, and cost from $200 to $300 per week.

One of the more reasonably priced modes of transportation is the bicycle (push-bike). There are bikes available for rent or to buy, or you can bring your own — which isn't a bad idea if you have access to good quality bikes at reasonable prices. The quality of ten-speed bikes available in New Zealand just isn't too high yet, and the prices are. Unless it's going to cost an awful lot to bring it with you, that's the best way to go. Check with your airline first to see what regulations you'll have to meet.

Bicycling (especially on the South Island) has become a pretty popular way to get around. Besides the low cost, you really get to see the country.

Hitchhiking is the cheapest way to travel and it's pretty safe and decently easy in New Zealand. There are places that are really hard to get to because of the lack of traffic — and remember that gas is expensive so people drive **little** cars and often don't have room for a person with lots of gear.

It's a terrific way to meet people, but hitching can be time-consuming if you have to wait a long time between rides. A few hints: Always try to look clean and somewhat respectable (but don't do it up too well — they'll figure you can afford the bus!). Be sure to pick a place where cars can stop safely and see you from a distance (beware of corners and hills). Signs saying where you're from, or the name of the place where you want to go sometimes help (especially if you're from out of the country).

Bus Routes and Fares

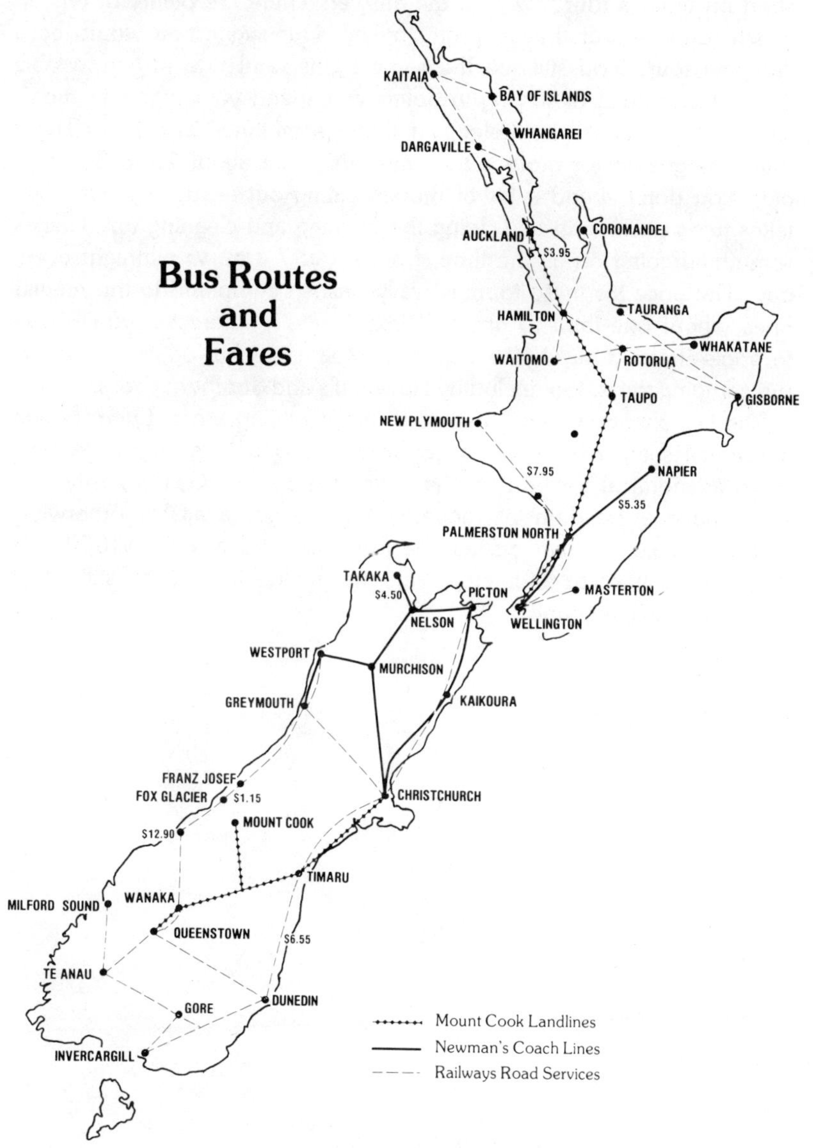

Lots of people go to New Zealand and figure that since it's not very big, they don't need much time to see it all. Wrong. But if you are short on time, a tour might be the answer. There are plenty of regular coach tours — but they're pretty pricey. Our suggestion would be a camping tour. You still see the same sights, and ride in comfortable buses, but instead of staying in hotels you spend your nights in motor camps. Sometimes you'll sleep in tents, sometimes in cabins. These tours are geared for more active travelers, from about 18 to 30 years old. You don't spend a lot of money eating out — usually everyone takes turns pitching in and doing the cooking and cleaning up. There's something going on all the time, from about 7 a.m. to midnight every day. The price for these tours is really slashed compared to the regular ones, about one-third to one-half less! If you're interested you'll have to book ahead. Our choice would be Moa Trek, but other companies run camping tours, too, including Newman's and Southern Cross.

The last alternative we'll mention here is buying a car. Even though automobiles are expensive, if you're planning a long stay it may be more economical for you to buy a good used car. Gas is costly, but you'll have a freedom of movement that's not available otherwise. Good, reliable cars can usually be purchased for around $1000, but they can be hard to find. However, that makes it easier to sell when you're leaving the country.

ACCOMMODATIONS

There are five major types of accommodation available in New Zealand. We'll cover three of these in each of the later chapters under **Places to Stay**, the other two types are usually too rich for our wallets.

Hostels are one of the really cheap ways to have a roof over your head, and a place to meet fellow travelers as well. They usually have cooking facilities and showers, but you'll have to provide your own sleeping bag, dishes, etc. The Youth Hostel Association is big in New Zealand — there are over 35 YHA hostels throughout the country. The YHA is affiliated with the international youth hostel organization, a year's membership will cost $10, and you can purchase memberships at any of the hostels. Nightly charges are from $2 to $3. The main drawback is that many hostels have curfews, and all are closed from 10 a.m. to 5 p.m. — so no sleeping in! Hostelling is popular, so it's a good idea to book ahead, especially in the summer.

The YMCAs and YWCAs in many cities have hostels (often no cooking facilities, though) and there are some private hostels, too.

Motor camps are the other cheap alternative, especially if you have a tent. Tenters usually pay from $1.25 to $2 per night, with use of all the facilities. These facilities include kitchens and showers, and often dining areas and TV rooms. As with hostels, you have to provide your own bedding and dishes.

If you don't have a tent, don't count motor camps out — most of them have cabins for rent. They range from rooms with bunks to little houses complete with kitchens. The prices are usually from $5 to $10 a night for two people and you'll need bedding and dishes here, too. A word to the wise, book ahead! Cabins are often booked months in advance by enterprising New Zealanders, so don't expect to land one at 6 p.m. during school holidays.

Bed and Breakfasts are the other budget accommodation. Just as the name suggests, you get a bed and breakfast — usually from $8 to $10 a night. Some B&Bs are in private homes, offering only a few rooms, others are Private Hotels accommodating 50 or 60 people. If you like a hearty breakfast to start the day out, as well as a nice bed with sheets to sleep on (and a private room) — this is the way to go.

The other two types of accommodation are motels and hotels — and both are usually too expensive to be called "budget". Motels normally start around $15 to $20 and hotels are about $20 and up. Both provide full service, full facilities, and full prices.

Sika deer, much smaller than the more common red deer, were introduced in 1905. They're found on the North Island, especially in the Kaimanawa Ranges.

FOOD AND DINING OUT

The fast-food franchises have made it to New Zealand, but you usually don't have to look too far to find something better. There are five basic types of eateries here (excluding the fff's).

Takeaway bars are what they sound like — you walk up to a counter, order your food, then take it away and eat it somewhere else. They usually have a variety of grilled and deep-fried food, from hamburgers to fish and chips.

Coffee lounges and tea rooms are normally "serve youself" but they provide tables to eat at. They have hot pies, sandwiches, grilled foods, and sometimes full meals. Unlicensed restaurants are the next step up, they sometimes advertise that you may Bring Your Own (liquor) and they serve meals, usually less costly than licensed restaurants.

Pub food is the name commonly given to the grilled and deep-fried meals available in taverns or hotel bars, it's also called "bistro food." Normally pub food is excellent value for the money — meals usually include meat, potatoes, and veges for about $1.50 to $3.

Licensed restaurants are the top of the line in quality eating, and the top of the line in price. Beware.

The other alternative we have to offer is to cook your own food. Most of the hostels and motor camps have cooking facilities, so this is the least expensive way to eat well. Particularly good buys are beef (although the prices are rising rapidly), lamb, and dairy products. Butchers, vege shops, and groceries are usually open from 8 a.m. to 5 p.m., Monday through Friday, and many dairies are open weekends, too. Dairies normally carry a limited supply of canned goods, some frozen food, and cheese, milk, eggs, and bread, so you shouldn't starve if you forget to shop on Friday.

Milk is probably the cheapest drink in New Zealand (next to water). A 600ml bottle (about a pint and a half, but called a pint) is only 15¢! The government subsidizes milk prices, figuring everyone can at least afford to buy milk to stay healthy.

BEVERAGES (ALCOHOLIC VARIETY)

So you made it through customs, found the shuttle bus into the city, and before you tackle anything else you'd like a tall, cool one . . . you're in luck, unless it's Sunday. You can buy your booze at a licensed restaurant (careful — it's pricey), a hotel, tavern, or for off the premises consumption at a bottle store or wholesaler. At the wholesaler you have to buy at least two gallons — but you can mix and match beer, wine, and spirits.

Bar hours are set from 11 a.m. to 10 p.m., Monday through Saturday, with some places open 'til 11 p.m. on Friday and Saturday nights. Sundays are dry, except at licensed restaurants and hotel guest bars. A guest bar in a hotel can only serve the people staying there — but they can order a drink anytime (as long as they can find someone to fix it). Cabarets, what few there are, are only in the larger cities. They have dining and entertainment and usually stay open until the wee hours of the morning (about 3 a.m.!).

Beer seems to be a mainstay of New Zealand life, and lucky for us, it's fairly inexpensive. A "7" (used to be 7 ounces, now it's 200ml) costs about 22ᶜ. A "handle" is a half-pint (imperial) glass with a handle on it — about 45ᶜ. But if you're serious about your draft beer, order it by the "jug" — 42 ounces for about 84ᶜ.

The wine industry in New Zealand is flourishing. The wines are not expensive, and the quality is really quite good.

If you go in for the "hard stuff," mixed drinks are usually plain (no blender-drinks or fancy-fruity types). Whisky and water, Scotch and soda, etc. But that keeps the prices down, 50ᶜ to $1.25 per drink!

The fantail is a protected native bird common on both islands.

WILDLIFE AND THE NATIONAL PARKS

Nearly all of New Zealand's land animals have been imported from other parts of the world — two species of bat are the only native mammals. Most of the animals have done extremely well, especially rabbits, deer, and opossums, while a few have had limited success (the North American moose, for example).

Red deer did so well, in fact, that until recently extermination-like procedures were used on them. Since an enterprising Kiwi discovered a world market hungry for venison, however, their numbers have declined rapidly — now deer farming is becoming an industry. As well as being valuable for meat, there is a demanding Eastern market for velvet (the male deer's antlers during the velvet season).

Wapiti (North American elk) have crossed with red deer — now there are few full-blooded wapiti left and they mainly inhabit Fiordland. The Virginia or white tail deer is found mostly on Stewart Island and there are some fallow deer in parts of the South Island. Tahr and chamois roam in the vicinity of Mount Cook National Park — in their 70-odd years they've also adapted well, to the point where shooting is encouraged.

New Zealand has some really strange native birds — the most famous is the onery little kiwi himself. There are three species, all nocturnal, all bad-tempered. They grow to be around 12 inches tall, about the size of a chicken. The tubby birds are tail-less and their feathers are more like hair than feathers. They hunt food at night — sniffing for grubs and worms with the nostrils at the end of their long bills. Mama-kiwi has it pretty rough — she lays a huge (up to one pound!) egg. But apparently feeling her duty is done, she leaves it up to papa-kiwi to hatch the egg and care for the youngster.

Unfortunately, the moa, a huge flightless bird that once roamed the grasslands of the South Island, is extinct. There were about 25 species at one time, the largest growing to over 10 feet tall! (The largest bird on earth.) Skeletons and reconstructions of moas can be viewed in many museums around the country.

The kiwi is the national bird, fairly common throughout the country. Plan on seeing him in a zoo, however, because his nocturnal habits make him hard to spot in the wild.

Keas are native alpine parrots that live in high rocky areas of the South Island. They are olive-green with brilliant reddish feathers under their wings and they have ferocious-looking beaks. Keas are terribly curious, with behavior ranging from funny (sliding down roofs) to destructive (tent ripping, etc.).

There is a "living fossil" in New Zealand called the tuatara. These lizard-like reptiles resemble miniature dinosaurs with their spiney-ridged backs. They are only found on the islands of Cook Strait.

Tuataras are often called "living fossils" because they are left-overs from the days of the dinosaurs.

Since the main native forests of the country take up to 700 years to mature (rimu, miro, matai, totara, and kahikatea) the Kiwis had to look for another kind of timber after the kauri stands were cut. They turned to the radiata pine, native to California. It grows 2½ times faster here, maturing in only 35 years. Kaingaroa State Forest near Rotorua is one of the largest man-made forests in the world — it covers over 374,000 acres. The scheme started as a make-work project during the Depression and has been growing ever since. The pine is very versatile, being used for all stages of house building, furniture, cardboard, and pulp. It is becoming a large export industry, too.

The giant kauri tree is native to New Zealand. It grows very slowly up to 170 feet tall and 50 feet around. The long straight trunks of the kauri yield relatively knotless wide boards, making it a very valuable building material. Unfortunately the early traders and settlers harvested most of the kauris — today the two major stands that are left are jealously protected.

There are absolutely no snakes here (although eels are abundant in some areas) and the worst pest you'll encounter is the sand fly. These awful little creatures can drive you crazy, so carry insect repellent when you plan to be outside (especially on the West Coast of the South Island. When it stops raining the little devils come out hungry!)

The National Park system is one of the oldest in the world and quite a few areas are protected by it. The North Island's three parks include Egmont, Tongariro (the first in the country, second in the world), and Urewera. The other seven are on the South Island.

Egmont National Park is the home of Mount Egmont. It holds the last of the dense Taranaki bush — has skifields and lots of good tramping.

Tongariro National Park's main focal points are the three volcanoes — Tongariro, Ngauruhoe (New Zealand's most active mainland volcano), and Ruapehu. The best skiing on the North Island is at Ruapehu, and all three mountains can be climbed. There are lots of good tramping tracks, too.

Urewera National Park is located in the Urewera Ranges. The density of its forests make for ideal hunting and tramping, and over 50 huts are available for use.

Abel Tasman National Park protects a part of the northern coastline of the South Island. Many of the activities here are water-oriented — skindiving, water skiing, boating, and swimming abound. There are also some good tramps.

Arthur's Pass National Park encompasses both sides of the Southern Alps, providing great contrasts in scenery and climate. There are a number of good tramps, and skiing at Temple Basin.

Fiordland National Park is the country's largest. Highlights include the many fiords and lakes. Well-known Milford Sound is within the park, as well as the Milford, Hollyford, and Routeburn Tracks.

Mount Aspiring also takes in part of the Southern Alps — it's especially popular with climbers and there are some good tramps. Althouth it shares a boundary with Fiordland National Park, its location rules out the amounts of rainfall common to Fiordland.

Mount Cook National Park is the home of New Zealand's highest mountain, Mount Cook, and many other peaks of the Southern Alps stand within its boundaries. Tahr and chamois are abundant as well as red deer. Trampers will often also see keas, native pigeons, tomtits, and riflemen. The park is the resting place for many glaciers, and skiing is a popular winter pastime. In the summer tramping and climbing take over.

Lake Rotoiti is the more popular of the two lakes in Nelson Lakes National Park, at least with the water skiers and boaters, but Lake Rotoroa has more brown trout. Water sports take precedence. Hunting for red deer and chamois is by permit and there is a skifield at Mount Robert.

Westland National Park encompasses Franz Josef and Fox Glaciers and ranges from the sea to the Southern Alps. Rainfall is heavy — but it's necessary to sustain the lush vegetation in the park. Tramping is popular, although the short trips to the glaciers occupy most visitors.

There is a good set of handbooks available — one about each park. The park headquarters can usually provide a wealth of information about nearly anything you'd care to ask about and the city nearest the park often has a park office where information is also available.

WALKING TRACKS (TRAMPING)

Kiwis love to go tramping — this is evident by the number of walking tracks you'll find throughout the country. There are five more popular, longer tracks that are all worthwhile. Try to do at least one tramp — if only to see what the tracks are like and to meet some people. They all have huts which are available for sleeping and cooking, usually a nominal fee is charged for upkeep.

Probably the most famous is the Milford Track in Fiordland National Park. It runs about 55km (34 mi.), from the head of Lake Te Anau to Milford Sound. It can be walked easily in three days, but many prefer to stay on the track an extra day to enjoy it at a more leisurely pace. Only a certain number of people are allowed on the track at one time, so you have to book ahead. Write to the Chief Ranger, Fiordland

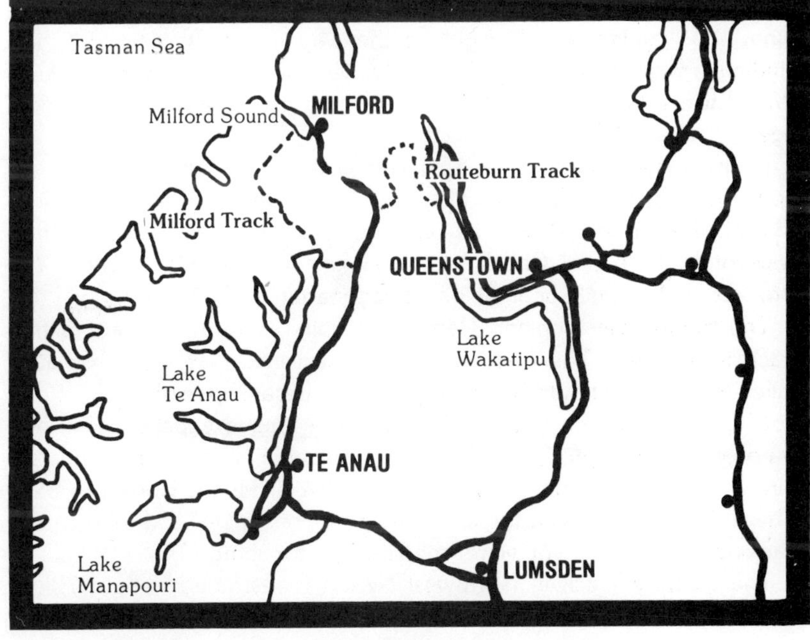

National Park, P.O. Box 29, Te Anau. There is also a "guided walk" (see below) so be sure to specify that you'll be a "freedom walker." Along with launch fees at each end of the track, you'll have to pay hut fees (the huts are spaced a day's walk apart) — the total is about $30.

For those who don't care to carry their own food or bedding and like to take showers and have meals prepared for them, there's a "guided walk" available. It is **essential** to book well ahead. Anyone from 10 to 70 can make the trip, write to the Government Tourist Office, P.O. Box 72, Dunedin, or see a travel agent. The cost? $150 to $210, depending on whether you take a 6 or 7 day package and whether you stay at the hostel or hotel at Milford Sound.

The Routeburn Track is probably the next-most famous, and more popular with some because all you pay is $2 per night for hut fees. The track is 40km (25 miles) long, takes three days, but you should allow four (the weather can get nasty). There are buses on certain days at either end to take you to the head of the track, or back to town if you're finishing the tramp. The Routeburn takes you through some beautiful country — mountains, waterfalls, and native bush. There are four huts available for sleeping and cooking — spaced at convenient intervals along the track.

Again, if you like the idea of not carrying your own food and bedding, the "guided walk" might be the way to go. It costs $95, including transportation to and from Queenstown. Write to Routeburn Walk Ltd., P.O. Box 271, Queenstown to book ahead, or try a travel agent.

In the same general area, you can walk the Hollyford. The track goes through the Hollyford Valley, you can probably make the 55 km (34 mi.) hike in four days. The only problem is that you have to either walk or fly back out! Check with Hollyford Tourist and Travel, P.O. Box 216, Invercargill, or at the park headquarters at Te Anau.

The tramp over Copland Pass is an alpine crossing — part of the track is over ice. There are three huts available over the 47km (29 mile) track, you should allow 3 to 5 days because weather can hold you up. Crossing the Main Divide can be a unique experience — but if no one in your group has any alpine experience it's a good idea to hire a guide from Alpine Guides Ltd. (either at Mount Cook or Fox). They'll provide you with the ice equipment you'll need and then cart it back out for you after you've reached the top, for about $15.

The Heaphy Track in Northwest Nelson Forest covers about 70km (43½ miles) and takes four days, minimum. The track follows the coast part of the way, starting 28km from Collingwood or 15km from Karamea. There are pay phones at both ends to call for transport (at Brown Hut and Kohaihai shelter). There are both huts and shelters available for public use. The Heaphy Track generally has less rain than those in Fiordland.

Common sense is the word for all tracks — sturdy hiking shoes and all-weather gear are advisable. You'll also need a sleeping bag, cooking gear, and food, and a first aid kit is a good idea.

There are many other walks all over the country, from ten minutes to days. By checking at park headquarters and public relations offices you should be able to find out what you need to know before attempting a tramp. So be prepared — and have fun!

You'll cross many rushing creeks and waterfalls on the R o u t e b u r n Track.

SPORTS

Both spectator sports and action sports can be found all over the country. There are many safe beaches for swimming and lots of good waves for surfing. Golf courses and tennis courts are abundant.

Hunting for animals and birds is good on both islands. Most native birds are protected, but the introduced birds and animals are usually fair game. Licenses are sometimes required, as well as permits — be sure to check (at a sporting goods store, park headquarters, or a PRO) before you take off. Deer and waterfowl are the most common prey.

Trout fishing in New Zealand is world famous. Both brown and rainbow trout have been introduced — very successfully. Salmon fishing is confined to a few rivers on the South Island. As with hunting, regulations differ in different areas, so check at a sporting goods store, park headquarters, or PRO for particulars.

Big game fishing at the Bay of Islands and Bay of Plenty lasts from December to May. Lots of world record class fish have been taken from these waters — blue, striped, and black marlin, tuna, yellowtail, and mako and hammerhead sharks.

Skiing is becoming more popular every year. There are major ski-fields at Mt. Egmont and Mt. Ruapehu on the North Island and the South Island has a number of fine areas, including Mt. Hutt, Coronet Peak, and Mount Cook. There is even glacier skiing throughout much of the year on Tasman Glacier at Mount Cook!

The more popular spectator sports include horse racing (there seems to be a track at almost every town!), cricket, and rugby (the national sport — much more brutal than American football!).

OTHER THINGS YOU MIGHT WANT TO KNOW ABOUT

Accidents: New Zealand has socialized medicine and coverage is included for visitors in case of an accident.

Automobile Association: The AA is really big here. If you're a member at home, be sure to bring your card, even if you don't plan on driving. You may be entitled to benefits like free maps, booking services, etc. The accommodation guides they put out are especially helpful.

Banks: are open from 10 a.m. to 4 p.m., Monday through Friday.

Driver's Licenses: To drive in New Zealand you must possess a valid license from Australia, Canada, the U.K., the U.S., West Germany, South Africa, Fiji, or New Zealand. The other alternative is an international driver's license.

Embassies: are located in Wellington, although some countries also have offices in Auckland.

Film: It's best to bring your own, because although it's available, it's expensive here.

Holidays: New Zealanders love their holidays, and have lots of them. As well as national holidays each province has an Anniversary Day. Summer holidays from school are from mid-December to the end of January and the kiddies are also out for two weeks in May and two more in August. National holidays include: Jan. 1 — New Year's Day, Feb. 6 — New Zealand Day, Good Friday, Easter Sunday, Easter Monday, Apr. 25 — Anzac Day, the first Monday in June — Queen's Birthday, the last Monday in October — Labour Day, Dec. 25 — Christmas Day, and Dec. 26 — Boxing Day. You can expect nearly everything to be closed on national holidays.

Information: Most towns of any size have a Public Relations Office (PRO) and the larger cities also have a Government Tourist Office (GTO). Along with the national park headquarters and offices, these agencies should be able to answer your questions.

Mail: If you want to keep in touch with home, have them send mail to you in care of the Chief Post Office in the city you'll be near. They'll hold your mail for 30 days.

Metric System: Here's a simple metric conversion chart:

Length: 1 kilometer (km) = .62 mile   1 mile = 1.609 kilometers
1 meter (m) = 1.09 yards   1 yard = .9144 meter
1 centimeter (cm) = .39 inch   1 inch = 2.54 centimeters

Area: 1 hectare (ha) = 2.47 acres   1 acre = .405 hectares

Liquid: 1 liter (l) = 1.057 quarts   1 quart = .946 liters
1 milliliter (ml) = .0338 ounce   1 ounce = 29.573 milliliters

Mass: 1 kilogram (kg) = 2.2046 pounds 1 pound = .453 kilograms
1 gram (g) = .035 ounces   1 ounce = 28.349 grams

Pedestrians: don't have the right of way except in marked crosswalks, be careful!

Rest Rooms: Almost every town has public rest rooms, otherwise try the nearest hotel (by the pub, of course!).

Shopping Hours: are generally from 9 a.m. to 5:30 p.m. Monday through Friday. Dairies are often open on weekends, and nearly every town or shopping center has a "late night" when they stay open until 9 p.m. (usually Thursday or Friday).

Part Two
The North Island
in Detail

BAY OF ISLANDS
(Paihia, Russell, and Waitangi)

Information: PRO — Marsden Rd., Paihia, ph. 683.

The Bay of Islands has some of the finest weather in all of New Zealand — all the better to enjoy the terrific beaches, cruises, and fishing.

Russell, originally known as Kororareka, was the first European settlement in New Zealand. The settlers were mostly ship deserters and escaped or time-expired convicts (from the penal colony at New South Wales). They and the men from the whaling and sealing ships that dropped anchor helped earn the name "Hell-hole of the Pacific" for the little town, but you'd never guess it by walking through placid Russell today.

The area also saw the first mission houses in the country (did they come to convert the Maoris or the first Europeans?). Waitangi is the famous site of the signing of the Treaty of Waitangi in 1840, which transferred sovereignty to the British Crown.

There are regular passenger ferries between Paihia and Russell, and a car ferry runs from Opua to Russell.

THINGS TO DO Cruises on the bay (which has some 150 islands) are a highlight of a visit to the Bay of Islands. The most famous is the **"Cream Trip,"** which began in the 1920s with a boat picking up dairy products and delivering supplies and mail to the farms on the islands. It's essentially a tourist run now, leaving Fuller's (as do all the cruises) at Paihia at 9:45 and Russell at 10:15, for a full day. The price is $8.75 (plus $2.50 for an optional chicken and champagne lunch). **The Cape Brett — Hole in the Rock Trip** is both exciting and beautiful, your launch actually goes through the hole in Piercy Island! It's a half-day trip, $7.50. There's also a leisurely **Champagne Cruise** for $6.50 (plus $2.50 for the optional chicken and champagne lunch). Or if you'd rather go your own way, see Bay Jets at the Paihia wharf about **hiring a boat.**

This hole in Piercy Rock is the destination of one of the cruises from the Bay of Islands. It's an eerie feeling when your launch creeps into the dark hole in the island and then bursts out amid the sunshine on the other side.

The Bay of Islands is famous for its big game fishing, thanks, at least in part, to Zane Grey, the famous cowboy novelist. The season here is one of the longest in the world — from December to May. They catch striped, blue, and black marlin, as well as tuna, yellowtail, and mako and hammerhead sharks — many are of world record size. It costs about $50 per day per person, but what a thrill! You can also go on a four-hour regular-type **fishing charter** for $8, including tackle, from Paihia or Russell.

For **flightseeing**, as well as transportation to Auckland, you can fly in an amphibian airplane with Sea Bee Air ($30).

In Russell, the **Captain Cook Memorial Museum** (30ᶜ) has a 1/5 scale working model of Cook's ship, the Endeavor, as well as other displays of a regional nature. The **Christ Church** is the oldest surviving church in New Zealand, built in 1836. And the **Pompallier House** has a collection of items pertaining to the mission here, 50ᶜ.

At Waitangi the main attraction is **Treaty House**, where the Treaty of Waitangi was signed. Also on the grounds are a carved **Maori meeting house** and a **war canoe.** On February 6 every year a ceremony is held on the lawn to celebrate the signing of the Treaty.

Alongside the Waitangi bridge, the Tui, a three-masted barque, is moored. The ship houses the **Shipwreck Museum**, with displays of all sorts recovered treasure, including the Rothschild jewels. Admission is $1.

Coach trips leave Paihia daily for destinations like Cape Reinga ($15), the kauri forests, and areas of historical interest.

PLACES TO STAY The nearest **YHA hostel** is at Kerikeri, but over at Russell you'll find the **Brumby Farm Lodge** (3km out on Opua Ferry Rd.). They have 50 beds in 4-berth rooms, with kitchen and dining facilities, for about $3 per person. Phone ahead for details, 704. Along the same line, but pricier, for a 50ᶜ booking fee the PRO will help you find a home that takes people in for bed and breakfast, but you have to book early.

The **Waitangi Motor Camp** is 1km from Waitangi, on the river, ph. 27-866. Tent sites are $3 for two and cabins are $9. The **Twin Pines Motor Camp** is 3km from Waitangi at Haruru Falls, ph. 27-322. Their tent sites are $4.20 for two people, cabins are $8. **Smith's Holiday Camp** is 2½km from Paihia on the road to Opua, ph. 27-678. They charge $2 per person for tent sites, $9 for cabins for two. Over at Russell the **Russell Motor Camp** is on Longbeach Rd., ph. 826. It'll cost $3.50 for a tent site for two and their cabins are $12.

FOOD In Paihia, **Momma's Delicatessen** has a chicken and salad plate for $1.50 to take away. The **JJJ Restaurant** has pies and baked goods to take away, but it's kind of high to eat it there. Over at Russell try the **Flower Day** for lunches, and the takeaway bar has homemade steak pies.

ENTERTAINMENT The **Waitangi Hotel** is usually busy in the evenings (and they have great orange juice) and the **Duke of Marlborough** at Russell has the distinction of holding the first liquor license ever issued in Kiwiland.

Other Spots in Northland

One of the most worthwhile tours you can take in New Zealand is to **Cape Reinga.** You leave from either Paihia ($15) or Kaitaia ($10) and spend a full day leaning back and looking at some fantastic scenery. Ninety-mile Beach (which is actually only 64 miles) is a stretch of unbroken sand — your bus will travel along it for about 45 minutes while you gaze at the sea (and enjoy the smooth ride). At Cape Reinga you can walk down to the lighthouse and see where the Pacific Ocean and Tasman Sea converge.

The driver points out other things of interest, both historical and odd, during the day. You can drive to the Cape on your own — but the commentary alone is worth the trip. (Plus the road is fairly poor in places — in fact, the stretch of road leading down to the beach is through a stream-bed and quicksands! $35 to get towed out!).

The other out-of-the-way attraction in Northland is the **Waipoua Kauri Forest**, one of the last extensive stands of kauri. These giants of the forest can grow to be 50 feet (15m) around and 170 feet (52m) high! They're a terrific source of lumber, and unfortunately the early settlers discovered that pretty quickly. In the early part of the 19th century kauri wood was the country's main export, and before long they had cut nearly all of it.

When the timber became scarce, men began to arrive to dig for kauri gum to export instead. Kauri trees give off a resin that hardens when it makes contact with the air — this is gum. The business was so lucrative for a while that it was called "kauri gold." Gum was used for jewelry, and also as a base for varnish and in making linoleum. To-day, synthetics have taken its place.

To get to the Waipoua Forest you take highway 12 north from Dargaville or south from Kaitaia. Once you get there stop at the forest headquarters, then take a side trip to see Te Matua Ngahere (Father of the Forest), 98 feet (30m) tall and 53 feet (16.1m) around, or Tanemahuta (God of the Forest), 169 feet (51m) high and a girth of 44 feet (13.4m). Both are fairly close to the road.

KERIKERI

Population: 1000. Information: Paihia PRO.

Although it's often grouped with the three towns of the Bay of Islands, Kerikeri has its own distinct beauty and character. It's a really artsy-craftsy area, and many of the local potters and weavers enjoy talking to customers and interested visitors about their crafts.

Kerikeri is also a citrus fruit growing center. During the main harvest season (June to February) the area bustles. Lots of oranges, mandarins, grapefruit, passion fruit, fejoas, lemons, tamarillos, and even kiwi fruit (Chinese gooseberries) soak up in the sun.

THINGS TO DO The oldest building in New Zealand, **Kemp House**, was part of the original Kerikeri settlement near Kerikeri Basin. Close by is the **Stone Store**, the oldest stone building in the country, which operates as a small store, with a museum on the top two floors.

Rewa's Maori Village, overlooking Kerikeri Basin, is a reconstructed pre-European village. In contrast, **Peacock Gardens**, between the township and the basin, has a post-European village.

Three local **crafts shops** that welcome visitors are The Black Sheep (spinning, weaving, and pottery), The Red Barn (pottery and handicrafts), and The Leather Point (leather goods).

If you arrange it ahead, you can pick up the **Cape Reinga bus** at the crossroads — but it's still $15.

PLACES TO STAY The **YHA hostel** is on Kerikeri Rd., ph. 660.

There are two campgrounds, one on each side of town on Kerikeri Rd. The **Aranga Motor Camp** is located along the river, before you get to town, ph. 224. Campsites for tents are $2 per person, and they have caravans for hire for $8. **Peacock Gardens** is about 1½km past the township, ph. 131. There are no cooking facilities or cabins. Tent sites are $1.75 per person.

FOOD **Bryce and Chapman** has health food takeaways and groceries and at the **Homestead Hotel** you can get bistro meals for about $1.50. **Adam and Eve's** offers a really varied menu in the $4 to $6 range if you're ready to splurge, if not, takeaways are available for lunch.

The wallaby, introduced from Australia, is found only on Kawau Island in the Hauraki Gulf, and near Rotorua.

WHANGAREI
Population: 39,000 (urban area). Information: PRO — Bank St., ph. 84-879.

Whangarei is the only "city" in Northland. Part of the reason is because there wasn't even an all-weather road between here and Auckland until the 1930s. The economy of Northland is based on sheep and cattle, dairy farming, and citrus orchards, with an oil refinery and power station at Whangarei. Other industries nearby include a fertilizer plant, sheet glassworks, and cement plant.

Whangarei has a sheltered harbor — between that and the mild climate it has become a favorite stopping place for yachties arriving in and departing from New Zealand. It's a good place for non-yachties to learn a little about sailing, too.

THINGS TO DO The **Clapham Clock Collection** is housed at 48 Vine St. There are over 400 clocks on display — the din on the hour is worth the visit!

Whangarei Falls is 3 miles from town on the road to Ngunguru. The falls make an impressive 80 foot (24m) drop, and are really beautiful. On the way out there stop at the **A. H. Reed Kauri Forest** and take a walk through the small stands of kauri trees (1½km from town).

There are chartered **launch and fishing trips**, and **coach tours** throughout Northland, check with the PRO.

PLACES TO STAY The **YHA hostel** is at 52 Punga Grove Ave., ph. 88-954.

There are lots of motor camps close to town. The closest is the **Alpha Caravan Park**, at 32 Tarewa Rd., ph. 89-867. It's ¾km from the p.o., close to the Main North Road. Tent sites are $4.50 for two and cabins are $8. Adjacent to Mair Park you'll find the **William Jones Park** (2½km from the p.o.) ph. 87-846. They haven't got cabins — tent sites are $1.50 per person. On the main road into town from Auckland, 3½km south, you'll pass the **Otaika Motor Lodge Caravan Park** at 136 Otaika Rd., ph. 81-163. Tent sites are $4 for two people and cabins start at $12. They have a swimming pool. Out at Whangarei Falls, 5km from town, you'll find the **Whangarei Falls Motor Camp**, ph. 70-609. Their tent sites are $3.80 for two, with cabins from $7.50.

There is only one place to get bed and breakfast — the **Hotel Windsor**, 2 Walton St., ph. 84-581, $10. At the **Whangarei Hotel** on Cameron St. it'll be $13 for a bed only, ph. 83-739.

FOOD The **Pizza Parlour** at 22 James St. has real pizza — complete with mozzarella cheese! (And it's terrific!) At the **Whangarei Hotel** meals start at about $2, and the **Settlers Tavern** has bistro food.

AUCKLAND

Population: 300,000 (750,000 urban area). Information: PRO — 6 Queen St., ph. 31-889 or GTO — 99 Queen St., ph. 798-180.

In one word, Auckland is **big**. Our advice, if you're arriving and departing through Auckland, is to stay only long enough to get over your jet lag and then take off. You'll appreciate what the city has to offer a lot more after seeing the rest of the country. New Zealand's largest metropolitan area can be a good friend or an utterly confusing experience — don't hesitate to ask questions. Remember that in general, Kiwis are friendly and helpful, even in the big city.

On fine days you'll see yachts (sailboats) sailing all over Waitemata Harbor and among the islands of the Hauraki Gulf — one annual event not to be missed is the Anniversary Day Regatta, the largest one-day boating event in the world. It takes place around the end of January and dates back all the way to 1840.

If you'd like to go for a boat ride — ask around nicely at the docks — maybe someone will take you out for a spin. Or go down to the Ferry Buildings at the foot of Queen St., from there you can take hydrofoil, launch, or ferry rides to any number of destinations.

Being nearly surrounded by water (Auckland got its start on the narrow isthmus for strategic reasons) it makes sense that there are many good beaches near the city. Some favorites are Takapuna and Milford on the North Shore, and Judges Bay and Mission Bay closer-in. There are even salt-water swimming pools (baths) at Parnell and near the foot of Hobson St.

Queen St. is the main shopping center downtown. You'll also find lots of restaurants, banks, theaters, and pubs in or near Queen St. The trolley bus which runs the length of Queen St. costs only 15ᶜ and it's on an honesty system. (Something you wouldn't see in the U.S., unfortunately.)

The Harbor Bridge, one of Auckland's newer landmarks, was completed in 1959. Within 10 years the traffic flow had increased to triple what it was, and alas, the fine new 4-lane bridge was too small. What to do? Well, Kiwis are pretty inventive, but for this problem they called in the even-more inventive Japanese, who merely "clipped" two extra lanes to each side of the bridge, making a total of 8!

THINGS TO DO There are two publications you can use while in Auckland to find your way around and see what's going on, the *Auckland Tourist Times* (weekly) and *This Month in Auckland*. Get both at the PRO.

Even if you're not into museums, see the **War Memorial Museum**. It's in the Auckland Domain, a huge park within the city, with entrances off Park Rd., Parnell Rd., and Stanley St. It's free and you can easily spend a half-day looking at South Pacific artifacts, the incredible Maori Collection, antique furniture, a mummy, etc., etc. There's a planetarium with shows throughout the day for 30ᶜ. (A good place to get acquainted with the stars of the Southern Hemisphere if you're from the North.) The museum is open every day from 10 a.m. to 5 p.m.

While we're on the subject of museums — the **Museum of Transport and Technology** has a variety of working machines (a tramway, railway, vintage cars, war machinery, engines) as well as a colonial village and the remains of the first airplane to fly in New Zealand. (Only three months after the Wright Brothers!) It's on the Great North Road and open daily.

Just a few blocks further, on Motions Rd., you'll find the **Auckland Zoo** where you can see kiwi birds, wallabies, and all the other traditional "zoo" animals, many in natural-like settings. It's open daily, $1.60 admission.

For Saturday shopping head out to **Parnell Village**. The shops here have been renovated in a Victorian style — it's a fun place to poke around on any day. Unfortunately prices are pretty high (but quality is high, too!).

To get a good look at the city, the best vantage points are atop some of Auckland's extinct volcanoes. **One Tree Hill** is 600 feet (183m) high, used to be a very impressive pa (fortified village). **Cor-**

1. Ferry Terminal	6. Art Gallery
2. Chief Post Office	7. PRO
3. Municipal Bus Terminal	8. Cook St. Market
4. GTO	9. YMCA
5. Automobile Assn.	10. YWCA

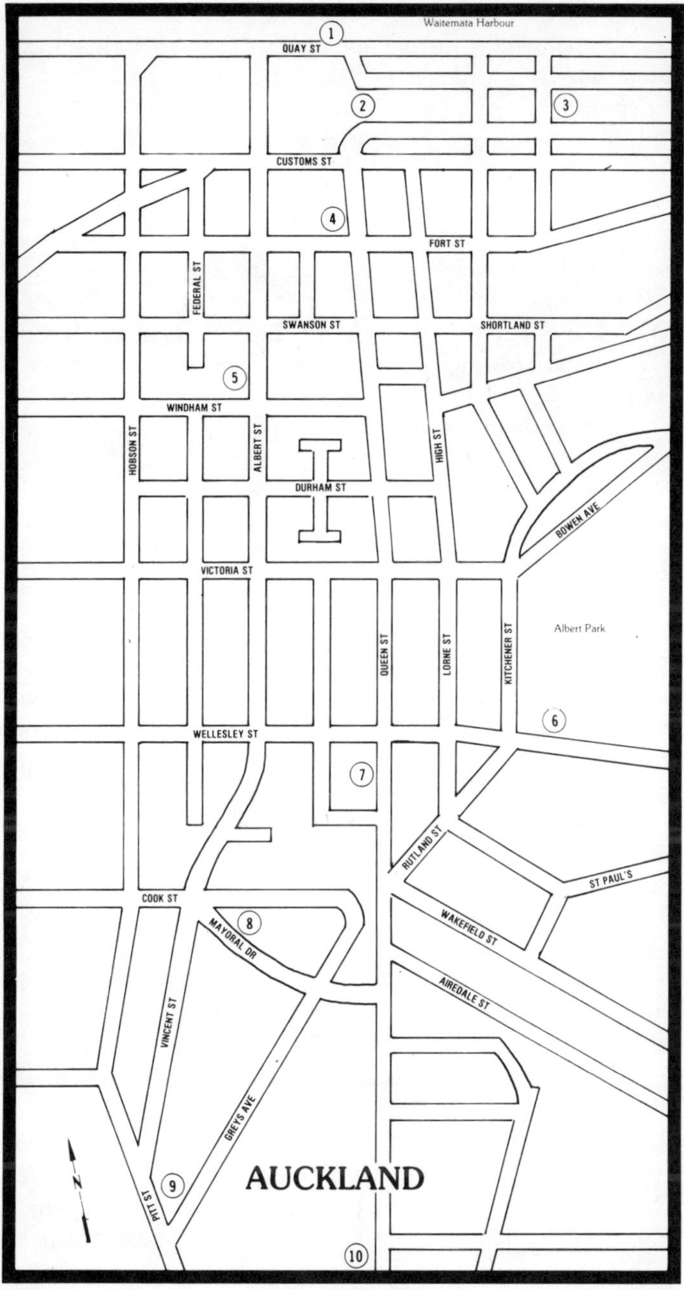

Waitemata Harbour
QUAY ST
CUSTOMS ST
FEDERAL ST
FORT ST
SWANSON ST
SHORTLAND ST
WINDHAM ST
HOBSON ST
ALBERT ST
HIGH ST
DURHAM ST
BOWEN AVE
VICTORIA ST
Albert Park
QUEEN ST
LORNE ST
KITCHENER ST
WELLESLEY ST
RUTLAND ST
ST PAUL'S
COOK ST
MAYORAL DR
WAKEFIELD ST
VINCENT ST
AIREDALE ST
GREYS AVE
AUCKLAND
PITT ST
N

nwall Park, near the base, has a herd of sheep and cattle grazing — an odd sight in the middle of the city! Access to the summit is from Manukau Rd., Greenlane West Rd., and Campbell Rd. **Mount Eden** (643 ft/196 m) was also a pa site, access is from Mount Eden Rd. The third major lookout is **Mount Albert**. To get there take Mount Albert Rd.

Albert Park is downtown, adjacent to the Auckland University campus. Only two blocks from Queen St., it's popular as a lunch spot for office workers and students, and a good place to get off the pavement for awhile. Nearby, on the corner of Kitchener St. and Wellesley St. E., is the **Auckland City Art Gallery**. It contains a really good collection of New Zealand art and a group of Gothic works dating back to 1300.

The **Auckland Observatory** is open on Tuesday evenings. It's located near the One Tree Hill Domain entrance off Manukau Rd. There are over 150 stalls with leatherwork, jewelry, food, pottery, artwork, clothing, and so on at the **Cook Street Market**. It's open on Friday and Saturday.

PLACES TO STAY There are four year-round hostels and one summer-only, plus three decently close motor camps, so cheap lodgings shouldn't be a problem. The **YHA hostel** is at 5A Oaklands Rd., Mount Eden, ph. 603-975. **Ivanhoe Lodge**, a private hostel, is at 16 Shirley Rd., in Walter Springs, take an 045 bus from Customs St. The rate per night is $3.50, ph. 862-800.

The **YMCA** at the corner of Pitt St. and Greys Ave. has rooms for men and women, ph. 32-066. The $10 charge includes breakfast and dinner. The **YWCA** at 385 Queen St. has rooms, ph. 78-763. The summer-only hostel is called **Boystown**, and located at 68 Nelson St., ph. 795-430.

The closest-in motor camp is the **Avondale Camp** at 46 Bollard Ave. (off New North Rd.) ph. 887-228. It's 5km from the p.o., take an Avondale bus from Virginia St. Tent sites are $3.50 for two, and cabins are $12. The **Takapuna Tourist Court** is 8km out, on Takapuna Beach, ph. 497-909. A Takapuna bus will get you there. Tent sites are $2.50 for two people and lodges are $5. The **Remuera Motor Lodge** is also 8km from the p.o., at 16A Minto Rd. (off Remuera Rd.) ph. 545-126. Take a Meadowbank bus to get there. It's $5 for a tent site for two people and cabins start at $11.

There are four nice B&Bs located really close-in. The **Arundel Private Hotel** is at 12 Waterloo Quadrant (next door to the Royal International Hotel) ph. 374-828, $9.50. The **Wakefield Private Hotel**, 72 Symonds St., ph. 771-039, is only $8. Also for $8, **Wellesley House**, at 74 Wellesley St. W., ph. 34-220. The **Railton Travel Hotel** is higher, $12.50, it's located at 411 Queen St., ph. 796-487.

FOOD Auckland is getting new restaurants all the time and you can find anything from good cheap food to health food to fantastic expensive stuff. In giving suggestions we'll stick pretty much to the downtown area.

For good vegetarian and health foods try the **Simple Cottage** on High St., **Cornucopia Health Foods** or **Peacock's Restaurant** in Vulcan Lane (off High St.), the **Belly Button** in the Canterbury Arcade near High St.), or **LeRoy's** at 78 Albert St. The food is all good and the prices are all reasonable.

Edoardo's La Tana Pizza Restaurant and Lasagna Bar is at 43 Victoria St. (They have fantastic lasagna!) Also in the Italian line, try **Pizzaroma** at 26 High St.

If you're just looking for a great sandwich we've got three places to recommend — the **Nosh Bar** on High St., **Crumb's Sandwich Bar** at the corner of Victoria and High Sts., and the **Upper Crust** on Durham St. (between Queen and High Sts.).

A really reasonable steak place is the **Red Grille Steak House** at 54 High St. — luncheon specials from $2.50 and for dinner try a steak, baked potato, and all the salad you can eat from $3.60! Terrific value. If you're looking for a good steak in a really nice atmosphere ($4 to $8) try one of the five Tony's restaurants: **Tony's Brittania** on Lake Rd. in Takapuna, **Tony's Lord Nelson** at 37 Victoria St., **Tony's Wellesley St. Restaurant** at 27 Wellesley St., **Tony's Lorne St. Restaurant** at 32 Lorne St., or **Tony's Duke of Marlborough** in Mission Bay.

Shopping in Parnell and having hunger pains? Try the **Alexander Tavern** for pub food, about $3. **Oliver's Expresso Coffee and Tea House** is a nice coffee shop, and if you're looking to spend more money try the **Parnell Steak House** — steak and salad bar for $5.50.

For something different you could try **Ali Baba's**, a Lebanese takeaway on Wellesley St. and the **Red Pagoda** at 178 Queen St.

has a Chinese-style smorgasbord all day for $3.50.

For pub food, the **Chef and Brewer** at 21 Elliott St. has meals from $1 and **Brewery Lane** at 246 Queen St. serves meals for about $2.50 or $3. The **DB Hotel** on the corner of Wellesley and Albert Sts. is also good.

ENTERTAINMENT Auckland is **the** place to be in New Zealand for entertainment. There are about a half-dozen cabarets, five live theatres, and lots of dancing and movies. Check the *Auckland Star* or the tourist publications to find out what's on and where.

Three downtown live-performance theatres are the **New Independent Theatre**, 2 Symonds St., the **Mercury Theatre** at 9 France St. (off Karangahape Rd.), and **His Majesty's Theatre** in His Majesty's Arcade off Queen St.

For cabarets you might try **Aladdin's** on Queen St. or **Charlie's Place** at 506 Queen St., they're both open 'til 3 a.m. A "different" evening is guaranteed at **Harro's Hofbrauhaus** at 16 Quay St. Sing along and dance to their "Oompahpah Trio!"

In Parnell there's live music at the **Windsor Castle** and the **Alexander Tavern** (a beer garden here, too). The **Cedars Restaurant** (Lebanese) has belly dancers to entertain their diners.

HAMILTON

Population: 95,000 (urban area). Information: PRO — Barton St., ph. 84-066.

The Waikato Plains are some of the richest farmlands in the world. Hamilton is located in the center of the Waikato, and is the country's largest inland city. The Waikato River, which flows through downtown Hamilton was once the main means of transport to and from the district. Today it's lined with parks and walking paths — a good place to escape the city's hustle and bustle.

THINGS TO DO Pick up *This Month in Hamilton* at the PRO for a list of the sporting events, exhibitions, and theatrical and musical productions.

    Hamilton Lake, on Ruakiwi Rd. offers yachting and boating, as well as miniature golf and roller skating.

    The **Waikato Art Gallery and Museum** houses a 140-year-old Maori war canoe. It's located at 150 London St. The **Hilldale Zoo Park**, off the road to Whatawhata, includes deer, wallabies, wild pigs, monkeys, big cats, etc. It is also a pheasant breeding farm — they liberate over 10,000 pheasants every year.

    Temple View, 4½ miles southwest of the city on Tuhikaramea Rd. is the New Zealand headquarters for the Mormon church. The complex includes the Church College of New Zealand and the Mormon Temple.

    Railways Road Services offers a half-day trip to the **Waitomo Caves** for $8.50. You can take a tour of the **Te Rapa Milk Powder Factory** on weekdays at 2 p.m. They process 400,000 gallons of milk every day at the factory on the Main North Rd.

PLACES TO STAY The **YHA hostel** is located at 19 Grantham St., ph. 80-009. The **YWCA** houses both women and men at their hostel at 28 Pembroke St., ph. 82-218. The $8 charge includes three meals.

    The **Municipal Camp** is 2½km from the p.o., on Ruakura

Rd. in Hamilton East, ph. 58-255. They don't have cabins, but tent sites are only $2 for two. A Claudlands bus will get you there, but they don't run on weekends. **Joyce's Motor Camp** is also 2½km from the p.o., in Hamilton East. It's on Cameron Rd., ph. 66-220. Take a Peachgrove St. bus (no weekend service). Tent sites are $2 per person and cabins start at $6.

The **Hillcrest Hostel** is also on Cameron Rd., ph. 63-462. It's only $7.50 for B&B. The two downtown B&Bs are **Riverview**, at 60 Victoria St., ph. 83-986, $8, and the **Parklands Travel Hotel** at 24 Bridge St., ph. 82-461, $9.

FOOD **La Brioche** on Alma St. has terrific homemade cakes and soups, they also serve sandwiches and hot pies. Also on Alma St. you'll find **Pizza and Pancakes** — both are good and inexpensive. If you want pub food the **Commercial Hotel** on Victoria St. has lunches for a dollar.

ENTERTAINMENT The **Hillcrest Tavern** on Clyde St. in Hamilton East has live music nightly. The cover charge depends on the band's reputation.

Waitomo Caves

The Waitomo Caves are 12 miles (19km) northwest of Te Kuiti, or 46 miles (74km) south of Hamilton. Buses and tours go to Waitomo from both towns, as well as from Rotorua and others further away. The reason 100,000 people every year go to Waitomo is the caves (there's not much else here). There are three main caves, each with a different nature.

The most popular, the **Waitomo Cave**, features limestone formations and an underground boat ride through a glowworm grotto for $2.50. The largest is the **Ruakuri Cave**, filled with weird caverns and a hidden waterfall, $1.25. The smallest and most beautiful is the **Aranui Cave**, which has delicate limestone formations, $1.25. You can buy a package ticket for all three caves for $4.50 (save 50ᶜ). Tickets are on sale at the Waitomo Tavern. Each tour lasts about 45 minutes.

Glowworms are fascinating little creatures. They're the larva stage of small fungus flies, about one inch long. Many sticky threads are suspended from the glowworm's hollow tube house, and when a flying insect is attracted by his light, it becomes trapped on the threads. He then hauls it up and eats it or stores it for a later meal. After about 9 months the glowworm becomes an adult fly. Time is running out, however, he only has about four days to mate and then he dies. Some unfortunates don't even last that long . . . not being much good in the memory department, they often see those pretty little lights belonging to their glowworm buddies and stop by to say, "Hi!" — and end up as dinner!

There's a campground, a small hostel (the Hamilton Tomo Group Hut), and a THC hotel at Waitomo. A small store has food to cook your own — otherwise you'll pay dearly at the THC for an a la carte dinner.

ROTORUA

Population: 46,000 (urban area). Information: PRO — Haupapa St., ph. 84-067 or GTO — 67 Fenton St., ph. 85-179.

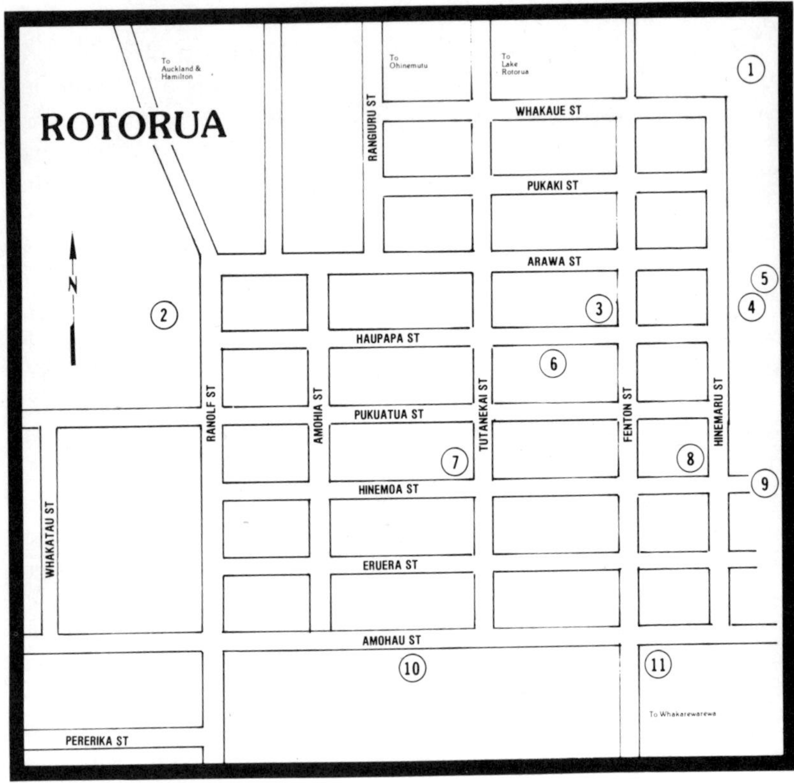

1. Government Gardens
2. Kuirau Park
3. GTO
4. Blue Baths
5. Tudor Towers, Museum
6. PRO
7. Chief Post Office
8. AA Office
9. Polynesian Pools
10. Railway Station
11. Maori Cultural Theatre

Rotorua is a wonderland of volcanic activity and Maori culture — soak in hot pools, watch geysers erupt and mud pools bubble, and learn about the native New Zealanders while enjoying a show put on by talented artists.

Many of Rotorua's residents have tapped the underground steam supplies and use it in their homes for heating, cooking, and even private hot pools. One of the first things a visitor will notice about the area, however, is the foul smell. It's a sulphuric odor — "rotten eggs" come to mind. After a few days most people get used to it.

There are four main thermal areas near Rotorua, and each one has a distinctive character. The closest is **Whakarewarewa** (Whaka-ree-wa-ree-wa) or Whaka for those of us having trouble with the Maori tongue twisters. It is a Maori village where they use the hot pools for cooking, washing clothes, bathing, and heating. There are seven active geysers on the silica terrace, the largest is Pohutu, which erupts up to 100 feet. (New Zealand's largest geyser.) There are also mud pools, a model pa, and a meeting house. It's open from 8:30 to 5:30 daily for tours. Adjacent to the reserve is the Maori Arts and Crafts Institute where you can watch carvers work with greenstone and wood, and see weaving and other craftwork. The workers are busy on weekdays only.

Tikitere is the most active area — it's also known as **Hell's Gate**. The mud pools bubble furiously and there's a hot waterfall. It's 11 miles (17½km) east, open 9 a.m. to 5 p.m. daily.

Waimangu is near the site of the 1886 Mt. Tarawera eruption. The mountain, supposedly extinct, erupted one June morning without any warning, obliterating three Maori villages and killing over 150 people. The roar was heard in Christchurch! The Waimangu Caldron within the grounds is a boiling lake of over 10 acres. Waimangu is 12 miles (19km) south of Rotorua on the main Taupo road, open during daylight hours.

The other thermal area is **Waiotapu**, the most colorful. The Artist's Palette is a three-acre silica terrace representing nearly every color, and Bridal Veil Falls vary from pinkish to gold. You'll find Waiotapu 19 miles (30½km) south on the main Taupo road, it's open during daylight hours. They also provide areas for free hot swims.

The other main Maori village in the area is **Ohinemutu**. It's located ½ mile from the p.o. on the lakeshore. The church on the site (St. Faith's Anglican) has lots of Maori carving and tukutuku panels, and there's also a sand-blasted window showing Christ dressed in a korowai (chief's cloak). It's placement gives the allusion of Christ walking on the waters of Lake Rotorua. The meeting house on the grounds is the site of a nightly cultural show, at 8 p.m. It's really informative and great fun (the young performers seem to have as much of a good time putting the concert on as the audience does watching) and only costs $2.

Besides a cultural show, every visitor to Rotorua should go to a hangi — hang the expense! A hangi is a Maori feast (actually the "hangi" is the underground steam oven used to cook the food). Hot river rocks are put into a big hole in the ground, then the food (in baskets) is placed on top of the rocks and covered with wet cloths and earth. After about two or three hours the meal is steamed to perfection, and delicious.

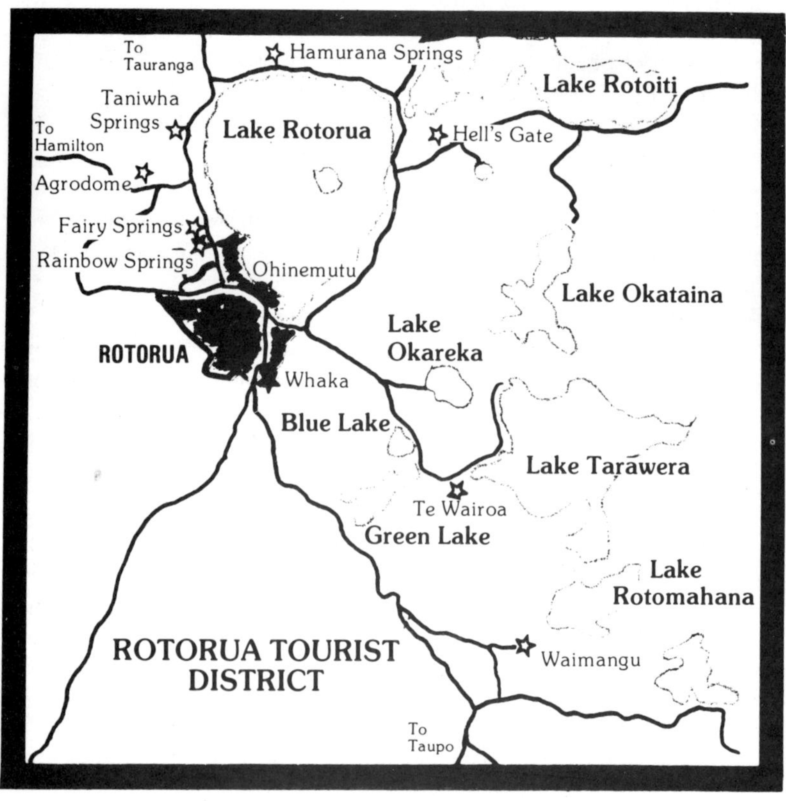

The hangi at the Rotorua International Hotel on Sunday nights is considered the best — $10 includes a fabulous "all you can eat" feast and a Maori concert afterward. The Geyserland Hotel has a hangi and concert on Wednesdays. Also check with the Travelodge and Tudor Towers about concerts and hangis. Traditional hangi food includes venison, kumaras, wild pork, smoked eel, raw fish, mussels, Maori bread, and chicken. You'll probably also have salads and fruit, and maybe lamb or ham, too.

THINGS TO DO Pick up *Thermalair*, the holiday newspaper and *This Week in Rotorua* to find out what's going on during your stay.

Besides the places already mentioned, there are lots of other things to see and do. Starting in Rotorua itself — at **Government Gardens** at the end of Arawa St. there's an art gallery, museum, and Sulphur Point, a swimming spot on the lake. Nearby you'll find the **Polynesian Pools**, which include public and private pools, mineral springs, massage, and sauna — on Hinemoa St., open 9 a.m. to 10 p.m.

The cruise to **Mokoia Island** in the middle of Lake Rotorua costs $4, and includes both scenery and a historical narrative.

The **Te Wairoa Buried Village** is New Zealand's Pompei. It was buried in the 1886 Tarawera eruption and later excavated. Go nine miles (14½km) east of the city, it's open daily.

Scenic flights are available from three companies. See the city, the volcanoes of Tongariro National Park, Mt. Tarawera, or even White Island in the Pacific Ocean. Prices range from $5 to $80, depending on what you want to see. Another way to see **Mount Tarawera** is by 4-wheel drive vehicle. The trip lasts four hours and will set you back $12.

The **Agrodome** has demonstrations of weaving, spinning, shearing, and working sheep dogs, as well as displays of various breeds of sheep and dairy cattle. Shows are at 10:30 and 2:30 daily, it's located at Riverdale Park.

One thing we haven't mentioned yet is **fishing**. Rotorua has 'em, and lots of 'em, too. You can only look at the trout at Taniwha Springs, Paradise Valley Springs, Rainbow Springs, or Fairy Springs, and if you like to catch them, you're in luck. Fish on your own or hire a guide — check with the PRO. The trout fishing is supposed to be GREAT!

There are lots of bus tours leaving from the Railways Travel Center on Amohau St. There are two especially good ones available. The first is called the **City Tour** and includes Ohinemutu, Government Gardens, Whakarewarewa, and Fairy Springs. It takes a half-day and costs $7. (That includes all admission fees, so it's an okay deal.) The other tour is a full day, the **Waimangu-Tarawera Round Trip**. A coach from Rotorua takes you to the Waimangu thermal area and then you take a launch across Lake Rotomohana, where a short walk brings you to Lake Tarawera and another launch across to the Te Wairoa Buried Village. A coach takes you by the Blue and Green Lakes on your way back to Rotorua. Price is $12 and you buy your own lunch — but you see a lot of fantastic things and will probably think it was worth it.

PLACES TO STAY The **YHA hostel** is on Tarewa Rd., ph. 85-866. The **YWCA** on Te Ngae Rd., ph. 85-445, also has accommodations. **Ivanhoe Traveller's Lodge** is a private hostel at 54 Haupapa St.,ph. 86-985, rates start at $3.50 per night.

The closest motor camp is the **Rotorua Thermal Motor Camp** on the Old Taupo Rd. They have hot pools and a swimming pool — that's why it's $3.60 for a tent site for two people and cabins start at $8, ph. 88-385. **Cosy Cottage Cabins and Caravan Park** on Whittaker Rd. charges $3 for tent sites for two and $6 for cabins, ph. 83-973. **Rainbow Springs Park** on N.S.H. 5 is 4km from town, ph. 81-887. They have cabins from $6 for two people, but no tent sites.

Rotorua has lots of motels around $15, but not many B&Bs. The **Tresco** at 3 Toko St., ph. 89-611, is $8.50. The **Morihana Travel Hostel** is at 20 Toko St., ph. 88-511, $9. **The Bungalow**, 15 Hinemoa St., ph. 88-516, costs a little more at $12.

FOOD **La Pizza Forno** at 44 Hinemoa St. has reasonably priced pizza and lasagna. **Enoch's Deli** in the Geyser Court Mall has sandwiches and salads to take away. For something different, try the **Pancake Parlour** at 47 Arawa St. They boast "pancakes served 100 different ways." The prices are reasonable, too. For pub food try the **Palace Tavern** on Arawa St. where bistro meals are from $2 to $3.

ENTERTAINMENT   After you've been to a hangi and concert, if you still have a few nights to kill in Rotorua the **Top of the Towers** in the Tudor Towers complex at Government Gardens has a nightly cabaret that goes to 3 a.m. There's also a cabaret on Friday and Saturday at the **Four Canoes Inn** on Fenton St. and plenty of "dine and dances" in the larger hotels. For live rock music and dancing go to the **Palace Tavern** on Arawa St.

TAUPO

Population: 13,500. Information: PRO — Tongariro St., ph. 89-002.

Lake Taupo is a fisherman's paradise, with trout averaging about 4½ pounds being common and many of the fish caught are at least twice that! Fishing from the shore and from boats are both popular — there's always good fishing somewhere on Taupo. The PRO can get you information on licenses, rods, tackle, boats, and guides.

The trout in New Zealand were introduced — brown trout from Tasmania and rainbow from California. The situation has reversed itself now, and hatcheries send eggs to Australia, Britain, Europe, and even back to California.

Taupo is located near the southern part of the North Island's thermal area — the lake is even heated by thermal activity. The DeBrett Thermal Pools and the A.C. Baths are both close-in, and many motels have hot pools, too.

THINGS TO DO Taupo is an out-door oriented area — water-skiing, walks, tramps, swimming, and of course fishing, are all among the pastimes here. **Kaimanawa Tours**, ph. 87-902, can arrange fishing, white water rafting, tramping, hunting (deer, wild pigs, and goats), and scenic trips.

At **Huka Falls**, north of town, the Waikato River drops 35 feet in a spectacular white water display. A bit further on, the **Aratiatia Rapids** flow twice daily, 10:00 to 11:30 and 2:30 to 4:00. The rest of the time the water is diverted for use in the nearby hydro-electric plant and the falls are dry.

The geo-thermal power plant in the **Wairakei Thermal Valley** was the second of its kind built in the world. The information office there can arrange tours and explain how geo-thermal power is harnessed and used.

Flightseeing trips to the volcanoes of Tongariro National Park are available for $25.

PLACES TO STAY There is a summer **youth hostel** on Redoubt St., ph. 84-021.

Because Taupo and the surrounding vicinity is such a popular holiday spot, there are places to stay all along the eastern shore of the lake. We'll deal only with places close to town.

The **Municipal Camp** is on Redoubt St., ph. 86-600. Tent sites are $1.50 per person and cabins start at $5.60 for two. The **Auto Park** is 1½km from the p.o. on Rangatira St., ph. 84-272. They charge $3.25 for a tent site for two people, or $5 for a cabin. The **DeBrett Thermal Caravan Park** is further out (3½km) on N.S.H. 5, ph. 88-559. The charge for a tent site is $3 for two. The **Taupo Cabins** are 1½km from the p.o. on Tonga Street, a cabin costs $6 for two, ph. 84-346.

At Huka Falls, near Taupo, the Waikato River rushes through a narrow gorge and then drops 35 feet in a striking white-water display.

Bradshaw's Private Hotel at 130 Heuheu St., ph. 88-288 has B&B for $9. The **Hilltop Colonial Inn** is pricier — $14 B&B, 80 Ngamotu Rd., ph. 89-015.

FOOD

FOOD There's nothing outstanding here, basically takeaways and more expensive licensed restaurants. The **Melita Coffee Lounge** has homemade pies and you can get a reasonably priced meal at the **Rosanna Restaurant**.

ENTERTAINMENT

ENTERTAINMENT **Chequers** is a fully licensed cabaret, and somewhat expensive — but you get dinner, dancing, and good music for your money.

TONGARIRO NATIONAL PARK

Information: Tongariro National Park Headquarters.

Tongariro is the country's oldest national park. In 1887 it was given to the government by the Tuwharetoa tribe in order to keep the sacred area from being split up into farms.

The three main peaks can be climbed, usually in one day. **Tongariro** (6458 ft.) is the lowest, but most complex, with craters (some active), hot springs, and bubbling mud pools. **Ngauruhoe** (7515 ft.) is the youngest of the volcanoes, still a very symmetrical cone-shaped mountain, still active. **Ruapehu** (9175 ft.) is also active, its crater lake simmers.

In the summer you can tramp and climb, and in the winter Ruapehu is the North Island's busiest skifield. There are huts throughout the park for overnight stays, and plenty of good walking tracks. Stop by park headquarters (behind the Chateau) to get details.

Speaking of the Chateau, it's the THC hotel at Tongariro. Next to the Hermitage at Mount Cook it's the most famous hotel in New Zealand. The elegant old building is worth a look inside — even if you can't afford to stay there! During the ski season the bistro bar downstairs has pub food.

PLACES TO STAY The budget accommodations here are slim, the Skotel and the motor camp make up the entire list. The **Skotel** consists of a hostel-like lodge (with hostel-like prices in the summer) and chalets that are more expensive. The **motor camp** charges $1.50 per person for tent sites and cabins start at $5 for two (but in the winter you have to book a whole cabin, $10).

FOOD There's a really limited supply of food at the motor camp store, and it's higher priced than elsewhere. They don't have milk or bread, but sometimes you can get both at the cafe next to the tavern.

ENTERTAINMENT **The Tavern** is the place to talk to your fellow trampers and skiers, and the **park headquarters** has shows during the summer (talks about the volcanoes, slides, etc.).

Mt. Ngaurahoe, located in Tongariro National Park, is New Zealand's most active mainland volcano.

NAPIER

Population: 48,000. Information: PRO — Marine Parade & Tennyson St., ph. 57-182.

The 1931 Hawke's Bay Earthquake reduced Napier to rubble, causing damage estimated at five million pounds, and killing 250 people in Napier and her sister-city, Hastings. But the earthquake reclaimed 8360 acres of land to the city from the sea. This area is now the site of industry, farmlands, and suburbs, as well as the Napier airport.

Today Napier is the largest city in Hawke's Bay, and the port here handles shipment of produce from the province's rich farm lands.

THINGS TO DO To start with, pick up a copy of the *Hawke's Bay Holiday Guide* at the PRO. The Marine Parade, constructed on rubble from the earthquake, holds many of the city's tourist attractions. **Marineland of New Zealand** includes performing dolphins, seals, sea lions, penguins, otters, and marine birds. Shows are given daily at 10 a.m. and 2 p.m., it's open from 9:30 to 4:30. The **Hawke's Bay Aquarium** has all sorts of fish on display, open daily from 9 a.m. to 5 p.m.

The Marine Parade also has a boating lake, train rides, a kiwi house, roller skating, a salt water swimming pool, putt putt golf, and the **Lilliput Village and Model Railway** which took 25 years to build.

You can also visit the **game farm and trout hatchery** in Greenmeadows, or take **fishing trips** and **launch cruises** on the bay. The **Cape Kidnapper's Gannet Colony** is the only known mainland gannet nesting area in the world, you can go via land rover, tractor and trailer, horseback, or on foot. Check with the PRO first.

There are all sorts of tours and **factory visits** available in Hawke's Bay, from wineries and cigarette factories to sheep stations, dairy farms, and a tannery. The PRO has details about these tours and others.

The **beaches** at Westshore (4km north) and the Marine Parade are both patrolled for swimming.

PLACES TO STAY   The **YHA hostel** is in Clive, about halfway between Napier and Hastings on the main road, ph. 20-662.

There are three campgrounds close-in. The **Kennedy Park Camp** is 2½km from the p.o. on the bus route (just off Kennedy Rd., in Marewa), ph. 439-126. It's adjacent to the rose gardens and an Olympic swimming pool. Tent sites are $3.50 for two and cabins start at $5.50. The **Westshore Holiday Camp** is on the Main Rd., Westshore. It's a bit further out, 4km, ph. 59-456. Tent sites are $1.50 per person and cabins are from $6.50. The **Riverside Motor Camp and Caravan Park** is at Taradale, 6½km from the p.o., ph. 442-732. Tent sites are $1.50 per person and cabins start at $5. Take a Hastings bus to get there.

Because Napier is a holiday area there is a good choice of B&Bs. Three of the cheaper ones are all on the Marine Parade: the **Blue Water Hotel** at 111, ph. 58-476, $8.50, the **Oceanview** at 47, ph. 57-039, $9, and the **Hotel Pacific** at 102, ph. 58-747, also $9.

The **Kennedy Park Motels**, adjacent to the motor camp, start for as little as $12 single, ph. 439-126.

FOOD   The **Whole Earth Restaurant** on Dickens St. has a great variety of hot dishes, salads, sandwiches, and wholemeal munchies. The food is terrific and the prices are reasonable. At the **Underground Bar** of the Leopard Inn you can get a "ploughman's lunch" which is a huge wholemeal bun filled to brimming, for $1. You can also get decent pub food at the **Criterion** and **Majestic Hotels.**

ENTERTAINMENT   Napier has three licensed cabarets, **Bimbo's** and the **Silver Spade** on Dickens St., and the **Cabaret Cabana** at Awatoto. The **Leopard Inn** has various bars and entertainment.

HASTINGS

Population: 36,000. Information: PRO — Queen & Russell Sts., ph. 69-001.

Hastings is the second-largest city in Hawke's Bay and the "twin city" of larger Napier, 21km to the north. Napier's port handles the output from Hastings' numerous factories. One of these, J. Watties Canneries, is the country's largest cannery — in fact, it's the most diversified in the entire Southern Hemisphere! Leopard Breweries has a large plant here, as does Unilever. And over three million sheep and cattle are processed through the freezing works annually.

Hastings is often called the "fruit bowl of New Zealand" because of the vast orchards in the area. The climate here is comparable to the wine producing areas in Europe and the Kiwis are taking advantage of it. No less than five wineries operate in and around Hastings, producing everything from sacramental to fruity to dry wines.

Although the 1931 earthquake is often referred to as the "Napier Earthquake," Hastings also took the full shock of it. Eighty-eight people were killed, the main street was razed, and the damage was estimated at over one million pounds.

THINGS TO DO Winery visits can be really fun (especially when you get to the tasting room) and some of the closer wineries include: The Mission (which has the oldest vineyard in the country) located at Greenmeadows, tours at 3 p.m.; Vidal Wines at 908 Avenue Rd. E.; T.M.V. Wines on Te Mata Rd. in Havelock North is the oldest commercial vineyard in New Zealand, tours at 2 p.m. and 3:30; and Lombardi Wines in Havelock North, also on Te Mata Rd.

The PRO can help you to arrange a **factory visit**.

Te Mata Peak offers the best views of Hawke's Bay to be found. The road to the summit is sign-posted off Te Mata Rd. in Havelock North (3mi. southeast of Hastings).

Fantasyland is an amusement park designed for children. It includes train rides, boat rides, miniature golf, and even a "castle."

The gannet colony at **Cape Kidnapper's**, 21km east to Clifton, is the only known mainland gannet colony in the world. The best time to visit is from November to February, and permits must be obtained at the Clifton Domain Office or the Dept. of Lands and Survey in Napier. It's an 8km walk along the beach to get there, or make other arrangements through the Napier or Hastings PROs before heading to Clifton.

PLACES TO STAY The **YHA hostel** is located at Clive, halfway between Hastings and Napier on the main road, ph. 20-662. The **YMCA hostel** on Railway Rd. has room for both men and women, $5, ph. 66-265.

The **Windsor Park Camp and Caravan Park** is 2½km from the p.o., on Windsor Rd., ph. 86-692. Tent sites for two people are $3 and cabins start at $6.

The **Grosvenor Travel Hotel** at 1117 Karamu Rd., ph. 86-732, has B&B for $8.50. It's slightly less at the **Park Lodge Travel Hotel**, 803 Princes St., ph. 89-881, $8.

FOOD For pub food try the Nova Grill at the **Lion Tavern** on Heretaunga St. (sorry, that's about it).

ENTERTAINMENT There's a disco upstairs at the **Lion Tavern**, and live rock music at the **Angus Inn** on Railway Rd. S., in the Bird Cage.

<table>
<tr><td>1. Railway Station</td><td>4. Hawke's Bay Bus Co.</td></tr>
<tr><td>2. Railway Bus Depot</td><td>5. Chief Post Office</td></tr>
<tr><td>3. PRO</td><td>6. Newman's</td></tr>
<tr><td colspan="2" align="center">7. AA Office</td></tr>
</table>

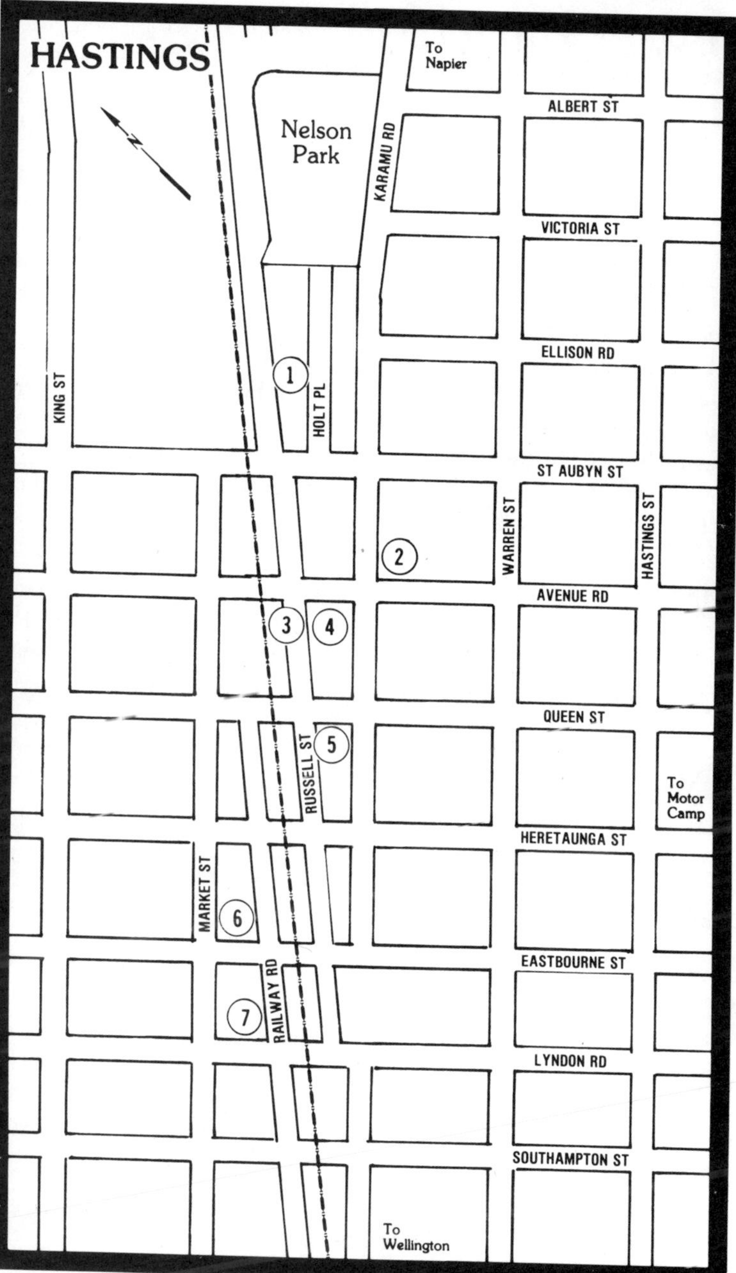

HASTINGS
Nelson Park
To Napier
KARAMU RD
ALBERT ST
VICTORIA ST
ELLISON RD
KING ST
HOLT PL
1
ST AUBYN ST
WARREN ST
HASTINGS ST
2
AVENUE RD
3
4
QUEEN ST
RUSSELL ST
5
To Motor Camp
HERETAUNGA ST
MARKET ST
6
EASTBOURNE ST
RAILWAY RD
7
LYNDON RD
SOUTHAMPTON ST
To Wellington

NEW PLYMOUTH

Population: 38,000. Information: PRO — Liardet & Leach Sts., ph. 86-086.

New Plymouth is the biggest city in Taranaki province, which contains some of the country's richest dairy lands. In fact, Port Taranaki is the world's largest exporter of cheese. The cheese-making process can be viewed on weekday mornings at the Bell Block Cheese Factory (on the Waitara exit from the city).

New Plymouth is a gateway to Mount Egmont, the symmetrical, snow-capped volcano that dominates the countryside. There are tour buses daily ($5.50) through Neuman's Sightseeing, and a special Sunday morning tour travels around the mountain ($14 includes lunch, and tea at a local dairy farm).

THINGS TO DO **Brooklands Park**, adjoining the beautiful **Pukekura Park**, is the home of the annual Festival of the Pines in January and February. The festival is set in the **Bowl of Brooklands**, a natural ampitheater that seats 17,000. Entertainment includes plays, musical nights, variety nights, etc.

The **Taranaki Museum** has a good collection of primitive Maori stone sculpture as well as the anchor-stone from the Tokomaru canoe which was part of the Great Migration of the 14th century.

St. Mary's Church (c. 1842) is the oldest stone church in New Zealand. It's located on Vivian St.

The observatory on Marsland Hill, off Robe St., is open on Tuesday evenings (weather permitting). A **planetarium** has recently been added to the complex.

The surf is usually good at **Fitzroy Beach**, about 2 miles east of the center, and **Kawaroa Park** has a temperature controlled

---

1. Road Services Depot
2. Chief Post Office
3. PRO
4. Marsland Hill
5. Kawaroa Park

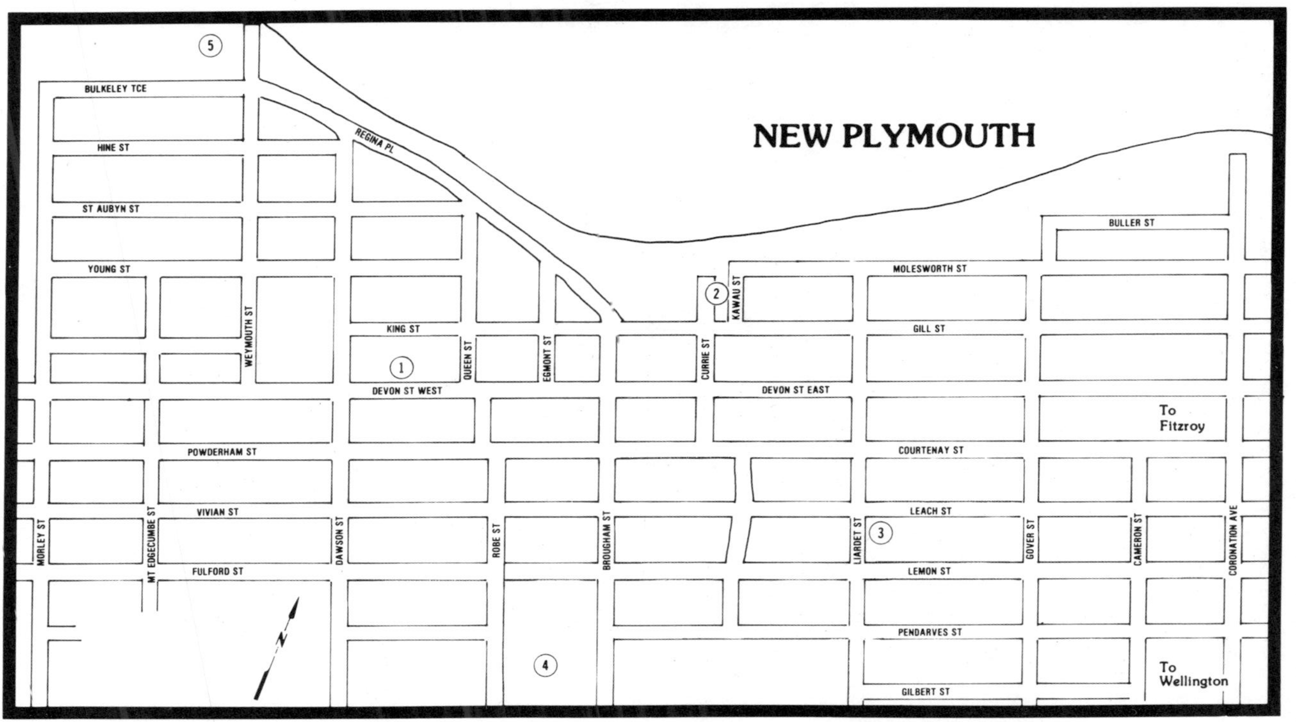
NEW PLYMOUTH
BULKELEY TCE
HINE ST
ST AUBYN ST
YOUNG ST
WEYMOUTH ST
REGINA PL
BULLER ST
MOLESWORTH ST
KAWAU ST
GILL ST
KING ST
QUEEN ST
EGMONT ST
CURRIE ST
DEVON ST WEST
DEVON ST EAST
To Fitzroy
POWDERHAM ST
COURTENAY ST
MORLEY ST
MT EDGECUMBE ST
VIVIAN ST
DAWSON ST
ROBE ST
BROUGHAM ST
LIARDET ST
LEACH ST
GOVER ST
CAMERON ST
CORONATION AVE
FULFORD ST
LEMON ST
PENDARVES ST
To Wellington
GILBERT ST
N

pool for swimming, as well as a diving pool. The facilities also include squash and tennis courts, and an aquarium (60ᶜ admission). The park is on Weymouth St.

PLACES TO STAY The **YHA hostel** is in Waiwakaiho Park at Fitzroy, 3km from the center, ph. 86-470. Take a Fitzroy bus.

The **Fitzroy Seaside Park** on Beach St. in Fitzroy is about 3km from the center, adjacent to the beach, ph. 82-870. Tent sites are $1.25 per person and cabins start at $6.40 for two. Take a Fitzroy bus. The **Belt Road Motor Camp** is closer to town, about 1½km from the p.o. on Belt Rd., overlooking Port Taranaki, ph. 80-228. Tent sites are $2.50 for two people, there are no cabins.

The **Princes Tourist Court Motor Camp** is 3½km from the center, on Princes St. in Fitzroy, ph. 82-566. Take a Fitzroy bus. Tent sites are more expensive at $3.50 for two, cabins start at $8. The **Huatoki Domain Motor Camp** is on Huatoki St., 3km from the p.o., ph. 35-092. It's open during the summer only, take a Vogeltown or Frankleigh Park bus. Tent sites are $1.10 per person with cabins from $6.50 for two.

There aren't many B&Bs, and the two we recommend both charge $11. The **Aotea Private Hotel** is at the corner of Weymouth and Young Sts., ph. 88-021. The **Inverness Private Hotel** is at 48 Lemon St., ph. 80-404.

The **Timandra Unity Motel** at 31B Timandra St. (off Coronation Ave.) charges $12 single.

FOOD The **Salad Bowl** at 211 Devon St. E. was originally a vegetarian restaurant. Now they also serve meat dishes, as well as salads, pizza, and wholemeal munchies. The food is reasonably priced, the taste is superb. The **State Hotel** on Devon St. has a $3 smorgasbord luncheon Monday through Saturday — it's nothing great, simply lots of filling food at a reasonable price. They also have family bistro meals from about $1.60.

Mount Egmont

Mount Egmont, perpetually snow-capped, last erupted in 1636. It rises 8260 feet out of the Taranaki plains.

There is a Maori myth that explains how Mount Egmont (Taranaki) came to be located all alone, near the coast. Originally Taranaki lived with the other mountains near Lake Taupo. One day when the mighty Tongariro was gone, Taranaki wooed his wife, lovely Pihanga, and won her away. But then Tongariro returned, surprising the guilty ones, and a terrible battle occurred, which Tongariro won. Taranaki was banished to his current location — he carved the course of the Wanganui River on his journey.

The climb to the summit is not difficult under favorable conditions, and the return climb can be completed easily in a day. Weather conditions on the mountain can change rapidly, so for the inexperienced, a guide is a good idea. Arrange it through the New Plymouth PRO.

There are three "mountain houses" that can be used as base camps for climbers, trampers, and skiers. Stratford Mountain House is 9 miles west of Stratford and close to the Manganui ski field. Dawson Falls Tourist Lodge is 18 miles north of Manaia (which is south of the summit). And the North Egmont Chalet is 16 miles from New Plymouth.

The nearest motor camp is at Stratford.

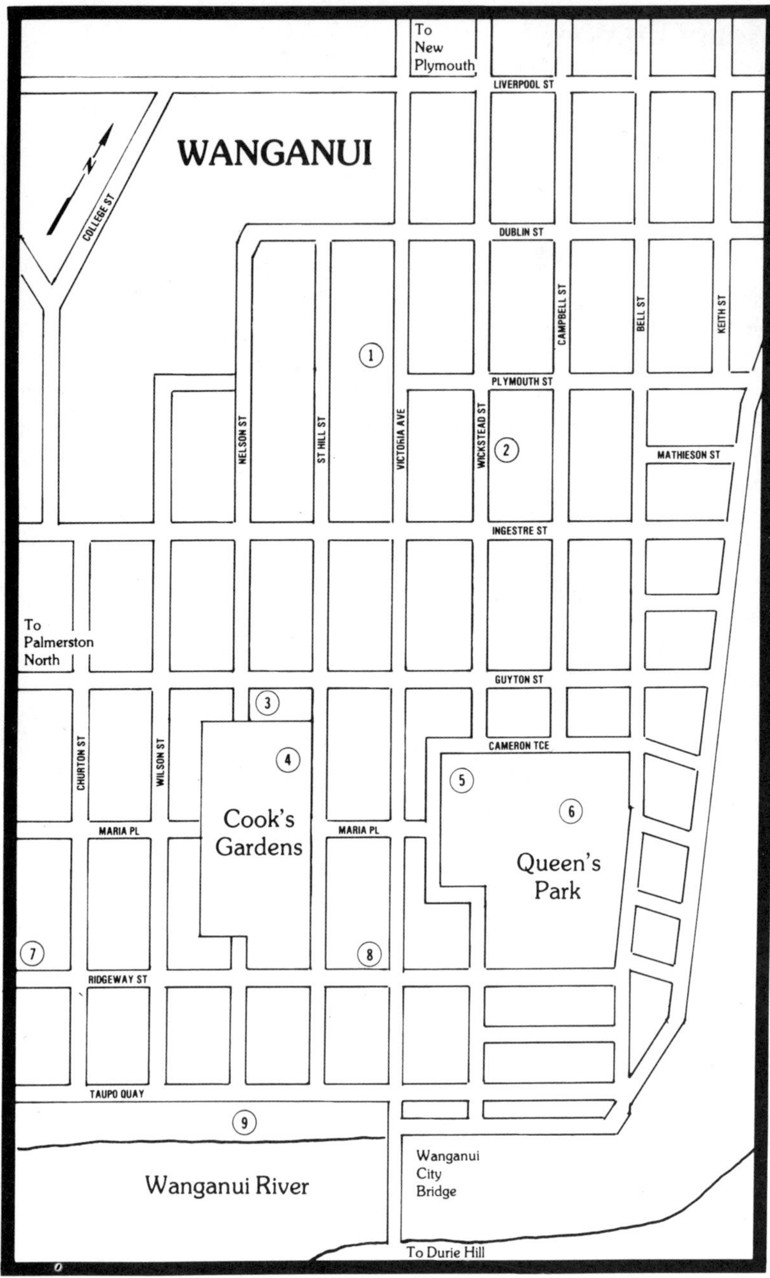

WANGANUI
To New Plymouth
LIVERPOOL ST
DUBLIN ST
COLLEGE ST
N
NELSON ST
ST HILL ST
VICTORIA AVE
WICKSTEAD ST
CAMPBELL ST
BELL ST
KEITH ST
PLYMOUTH ST
MATHIESON ST
INGESTRE ST
To Palmerston North
GUYTON ST
CHURTON ST
WILSON ST
CAMERON TCE
Cook's Gardens
MARIA PL
MARIA PL
Queen's Park
RIDGEWAY ST
TAUPO QUAY
Wanganui River
Wanganui City Bridge
To Durie Hill

WANGANUI

Population: 38,000. Information: PRO — Guyton & St. Hill Sts., ph. 53-286.

Wanganui is one of the oldest cities in New Zealand. The Wanganui River provided a navigable waterway to the interior, as well as a coastal port. When the European settlers came in 1840 they found a large Maori population, and after some initial problems concerning the purchase of land from the Maoris, the two societies became friendly and lived in harmony. The Wanganui Maoris, in fact, teamed with the settlers to head off a warring tribe during the Land Wars, and thus saved the settlement.

The town was originally named Petre, but the settlers persisted in using the Maori name and finally petitioned that Wanganui be adopted instead. Wanganui (originally Whanganui) is a disputed Maori name. It was first thought to mean "big harbor" because the river used to extend all the way across the valley from Durie Hill to St. John's Hill. Now, however, it's suggested that it means "long waiting" referring to a time when an important chief had to wait for a long time to be ferried from one side of the river to the other.

THINGS TO DO Wanganui River Jet Tours has **jet boat trips** up the river. You can go clear to Taumarunui, or if a more leisurely trip is your preference, take the MV Waireka, an old **riverboat**, to Hipango Park. Make arrangements through the AA office at 273 Victoria St., or call 36-346.

The **Wanganui Regional Museum** on Watt St. is the largest regional museum in the country. The Maori Court exhibit is outstanding — one of its main attractions is an authentic war canoe, complete with bullets in the hull!

1. AA Office
2. YWCA
3. PRO
4. Observatory
5. Museum
6. Sarjeant Art Gallery
7. Newman's
8. Chief Post Office
9. Railway Station and
   Road Services Depot

At the bottom of Virginia Ave. you'll find the **Durie Hill** pedestrian tunnel which goes 205m into the hill, you can ride an elevator the 216 ft. to the top. If you then climb to the top of the 100 ft. Memorial Tower, a commanding view, including Mt. Egmont, Mt. Ruapehu, and on an especially fine day even the South Island, can be seen.

Virginia Lake, on the Great North Rd., is a good picnic spot. The lovely gardens are complemented by an assortment of waterfowl. (There seemed to be an awful lot of ducks when we were there, bunches of them!)

The **Sarjeant Gallery** in Queen's Park is open daily, it includes mostly British and New Zealand artists. The **Putiki Church** (St. Paul's Memorial Church) on Anaua St. in Putiki is a fine example of Maori carving and tukutuku wall panels.

The deer in the park at the bottom of St. John's Hill may be fed by hand. You can visit the **Wanganui Woolen Mills** on Kelvin St., Aramoho, ph. 39-054. And the people at **Holly Lodge**, a small winery, will show you their operation and let you sample their wines (hoping that you'll purchase a bottle or two, of course!). It's about a mile past the Aramoho Motor Camp on Somme Parade.

The **beach** at Castlecliff is fully developed — it's six miles west of the city.

PLACES TO STAY The **YHA hostel** is located out at Castlecliff (about six miles from the city) at 3 Tregenna St., ph. 44-111. Take a Castlecliff bus. The **YWCA** at 232 Wickstead St. takes women only, ph. 57-480.

The **Aramoho Park Camp** is 6½km from the p.o. on Somme Parade, beside the river, ph. 38-402. Take an Aramoho Park bus. Tent sites are $1.50 per person, cabin charges start at $6 a night for two. The **Castlecliff Camp** is about 8km from town at the beach, ph. 45-817. A Castlecliff bus will get you there. Tent sites are $3 for two, they don't have cabins.

The **Cainbrae Private Hotel** is at 24 Somme Parade, ph. 57-918. They have B&B for $10. At the **Top O'the Tavern**, 75 Ridgeway St., ph. 57-831, it's $9.50.

FOOD **Dr. Johnson's Coffee House** in Tudor Court on Victoria

Ave. has a lunchtime smorgasbord — you pay per portion. **Shakey's Pizza Parlour** (not to be confused with the American franchise) is on the corner of Ridgeway and St. Hill Sts. The **Cuba Coffee Lounge** on Victoria Ave. has good lunchtime variety.

ENTERTAINMENT The **Four Seasons Professional Theatre** puts on about 12 plays annually. Phone 55-870 to see what's on at their playhouse on Main South Road. The **Grand International Hotel** often has a band.

PALMERSTON NORTH

Population: 58,000. Information: PRO — The Square, ph. 85-003.

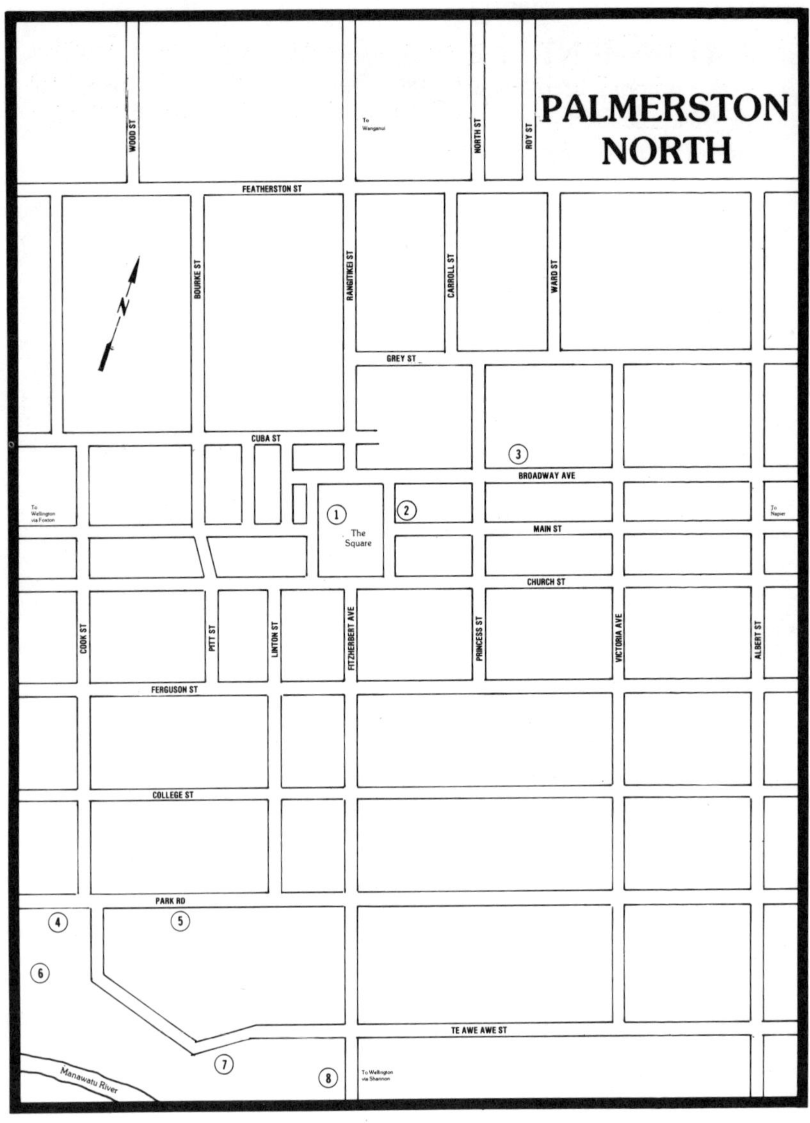

Palmerston North is an agricultural center. A great deal of research is carried on here at Massey University, the Palmerston North Seed Testing Station, and the New Zealand Dairy Research Institute. Visits can be arranged if you have an interest in these or other farming matters. Massey University is now fully autonomous, although it began as an agricultural college. It's the national center for veterinary sciences, food sciences, and biotechnology.

The center of the city is the 17-acre Square.

THINGS TO DO Pick up *Town and Around* at the PRO for details on what's happening in Palmerston North, it's published monthly.

The **Manawatu Museum** on Church St. consists of mainly regional matter, includes the first store in Palmerston North and an early homestead. The **National Rugby Museum** is of interest to those curious about the national sport — it's at the corner of Grey and Carroll Sts. (50¢).

The **Esplanade Gardens** is a beautiful reserve off Park Rd. The complex includes rose trial grounds, a conservatory, an aviary, a scented garden for the blind, a miniature railway, mini-golf, and botanical gardens. Situated near the Esplanade, also off Park Rd., the **Lido Swimming Center** boasts three pools, all temperature controlled.

PLACES TO STAY The **summer hostel** is at 74 Fitzroy St., ph. 68-374. During the rest of the year go to 40 Cuba St., or ph. 82-839.

The **Palmerston North Camping Ground** is about 2km from the Square, on Park Rd., ph. 80-349. Tent sites are $2.50 for two persons, cabins start at $4.50 for two.

Two of the more reasonably priced B&Bs are the **Ambassador Hotel**, 219 Broadway, ph. 86-371, $9, and **Grey's Inn** at 123 Grey St., ph. 86-928, $11.

1. PRO	5. Ongley Park
2. Chief Post Office	6. Motor Camp
3. Automobile Assn.	7. Esplanade Gardens
4. Lido Swimming Center	8. Fitzherbert Park

Palmerston North is a convention center, which explains the abundance of hotels and motels. The **Broadway Motel** at 258 Broadway, ph. 85-051, is $16 single, and the **Motel Sunglow** at 118 Ruahine St., ph. 77-481 is only $13 single.

FOOD Although the convention atmosphere of Palmerston North is good as far as accommodations go, that same convention orientation is probably the reason that there isn't much cheap food. You'll find the usual franchises (Wimpy's, KFC, etc.) take-aways, and a variety of licensed restaurants.

For good pub food the **Commercial Hotel** on the Square offers a choice of hot dishes or cold meats and salad for lunch, for only $1.50. It's an excellent value because the food is really good. The **Bistro Licensed Restaurant** on Fitzherbert Ave. is more expensive ($6 and up), but they serve delicacies like venison steak, pheasant pate', and snails. The prices aren't out of line at all considering the variety.

ENTERTAINMENT The **Centerpoint Theatre and Restaurant** on Church St. has a good reputation for their productions. The *Evening Standard* lists all entertainments on the inside back page.

A Maori meeting house, "whare runanga." These buildings are quite common throughout the North Island.

WELLINGTON

Population: 328,000 (urban area). Information: PRO — 2 Mercer St., ph. 724-599 or GTO — 80 Wakefield St., ph. 739-269.

Wellington, the capital city of New Zealand, is affectionately called "Windy Wellington." Wind is a fact of life in Wellington, and everyone just lives with it. Many compare the city to San Francisco because it's built on steep hillsides rising out of a beautiful harbor.

The main shopping street is Lambton Quay, which was originally the shoreline. All of the buildings on the harbor side of the street have been built on reclaimed land.

Wellington was settled in 1840, the first of the New Zealand Company's settlements in the country. For 25 years, the battle raged with Auckland over which city could best serve as capital. Finally, in 1865, an independent commission chosen by three Australian governors voted to move the capital to more centrally-located Wellington.

THINGS TO DO The *Capital Visitor*, a small newspaper published weekly is a good guide for Wellington. It's available at the PRO, GTO, and hotels. The *Capital City Calendar* is a monthly publication of the PRO, and lists meetings, exhibitions, concerts, and other things to do.

The **National Museum and National Art Gallery** are housed in the same complex on Buckle St. **Tours of Parliament** are conducted Monday through Friday, ph. 728-288. The newest building in the complex is known as the "beehive" for obvious reasons.

The **City Bus Tour**, $3, leaves daily at 2 p.m. from in front of

<table>
<tr><td>1. Parliament</td><td>5. Chief Post Office</td></tr>
<tr><td>2. AA Office</td><td>6. PRO</td></tr>
<tr><td>3. City Bus Terminal</td><td>7. Planetarium</td></tr>
<tr><td>4. GTO</td><td>8. Railway Station</td></tr>
<tr><td colspan="2" align="center">9. Picton Ferry</td></tr>
</table>

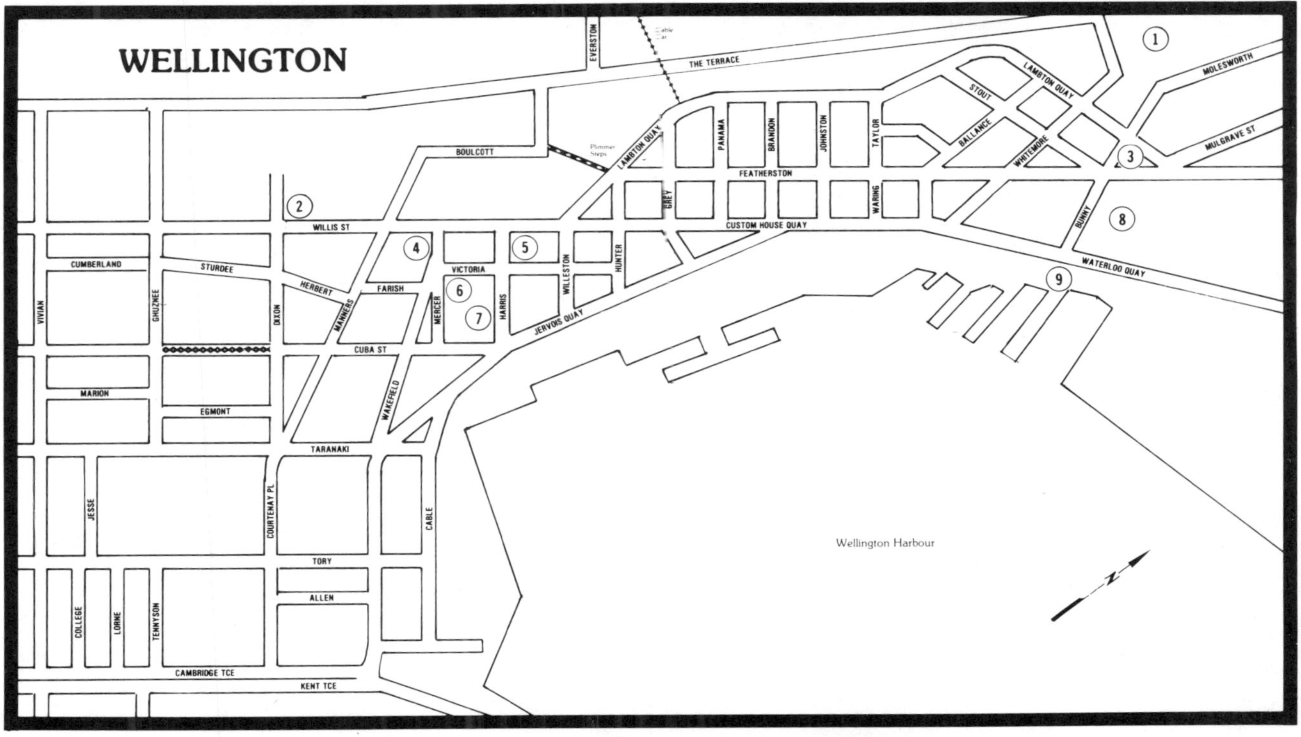

WELLINGTON
Wellington Harbour
EVERSTON
Cable Car
THE TERRACE
MOLESWORTH
LAMBTON QUAY
STOUT
MULGRAVE ST
BALLANCE
WHITEMORE
TAYLOR
JOHNSTON
BRANDON
PANAMA
FEATHERSTON
LAMBTON QUAY
Plimmer Steps
BOULCOTT
WARING
GREY
CUSTOM HOUSE QUAY
BUNNY
WATERLOO QUAY
WILLIS ST
HUNTER
WILLESTON
HERBERT
VICTORIA
HARRIS
JERVOIS QUAY
CUMBERLAND
STURDEE
MANNERS
FARISH
MERCER
VIVIAN
GHUZNEE
DIXON
CUBA ST
MARION
EGMONT
WAKEFIELD
TARANAKI
COURTENAY PL
CABLE
JESSE
TORY
ALLEN
COLLEGE
LORNE
TENNYSON
CAMBRIDGE TCE
KENT TCE

the PRO. It gives a quick once-over of the city to acquaint visitors with it. The view from **Mount Victoria** is lovely, and places the whole city in perspective. A highlight of the tour is the stop at **Old St. Paul's** on Mulgrave St. This church, over 100 years old, is a fine example of wooden Gothic architecture — it's really something.

The **Wellington Zoo** has birds, bears, bison, and all sorts of other animals including kangaroos, elephants, apes, etc. It's open daily from 8:30 to 5:00, 90ᶜ admission. Take a Newtown #11 bus — the zoo is on Manchester St., off Roy St.

From **Cable Car Lane**, off Lambton Quay, ride the cable car up to the **Botanic Gardens**. Besides the gardens, on the walk back down you'll see some great views of the city and harbor.

There are free tours of the **Radio New Zealand** broadcast center on Bowen St., ph. 721-777. **Scenic flights** and **harbor cruises** are available, contact the PRO. There are some nice beaches around, the closest to town is Oriental Bay. Plus there are golf courses, horseback riding, roller skating, etc.

PLACES TO STAY For a city of its size, Wellington doesn't have a lot of budget accommodations close-in. Many of the more reasonable motels and guest houses, as well as a YHA hostel and motor camp, are found in Lower Hutt, one of Wellington's "bedroom communities," about 14km to the northeast.

The new **YHA hostel** is in the city at 40 Tinakori Rd. (15 minutes from the railway station), ph. 736-271. Take a number 14 bus to Wadestown if you don't want to walk. The other **YHA hostel** is at 43 Pretoria St. in Lower Hutt, ph. 696-019. Take a commuter train to Lower Hutt. The **YWCA hostel** is downtown, at 355 Willis St., ph. 850-505. They accommodate both women and men, $8 for dinner, bed, and breakfast, $6.50 B&B.

The nearest motor camp is the **Hutt Park Motor Camp** at Moera, Lower Hutt, 15km from Wellington, ph. 685-913. Tent sites are $3 for two, cabins start at $5. Take an Eastbourne bus from Lambton Quay.

The **Railton Hotel** at 213 Cuba St., ph. 851-632, charges $11.50 for B&B. **Richmond House**, 116 Brougham St., ph. 858-529, is only $8. And the **Balcairn Private Hotel** at 151

Ghuznee St., ph. 842-274, only charges $9, but then they soak you another $1.50 for a continental breakfast!

FOOD The **Mexican Cantina** at 40 Willis St. has terrific Mexican food at moderate prices — the only Mexican food in Wellington, too. **The Touchwood**, on the Plimmer Steps (off Lambton Quay) is pleasant, has a salad bar. **The Kumquat** at 290 Lambton Quay is strictly vegetarian. For wholemeal foods try the **Sunflower Salad Bar** at 157 Cuba St., and for pizza, **Luigi's** is close-in at the corner of Vivian and Willis.

There's plenty of pub food, although it seems a little higher priced here. And if you feel like going fancy, Wellington has a good selection of places in the higher price ranges — after all, all of those diplomats have to eat somewhere!

ENTERTAINMENT There are lots of dine and dance restaurants. For movies and plays see the *Capital Visitor* or the *Evening Post* to find out what's on and when. The **1860 Victualling Co.** on Lambton Quay usually has some sort of music, as do most of the better hotels.

From Wellington to Picton
(Via the Ferry)

The 2½-hour ferry ride from Wellington to Picton is usually a beautiful, relaxing trip — although Cook Strait can come up with some foul weather at times. The ferry leaves daily at 10 a.m. and 6:40 p.m., with other sailings scheduled on some days, ph. 725-399 for information and car reservations.

The two ferries, Aramoana (great pathway across the sea) and Aranui (great pathway) both have lounges, bars, and cafeterias (although we suggest you bring along your own food if you have to eat). The fare is $7.60 per person, one way, but if you want to return the same day there's a special rate. Be sure to reserve a spot if you're taking a car across during the summer, it can get crowded.

Part Three
The South Island
in Detail

NELSON

Population: 33,000. Information: PRO — Lower Trafalgar and Halifax Sts., ph. 83-470.

Nelson is essentially an agricultural center — due to the fertile land and the abundance of sunshine. The area produces lots of fruit, tobacco, and all of New Zealand's hops. But it's also a resort area — once again, due to the sunshine, and the beautiful beaches. If you want to book lodgings in Nelson, be sure to do it well ahead of time, especially if you'll be arriving during the summer months or school holidays.

The **Riverside Community** (about 30 miles west on highway 60) is a commune that has been functioning with much success for nearly 40 years. Although founded by pacifist Methodists, membership is now open to "all who see life as religion, and all activity as worship." They own over 500 acres and raise livestock and crops, both for their own use and to sell. Each family has their own home and all members share the work. Over the years the Riverside people have become an integral part of the locality.

New Zealand's first rugby club was started in Nelson, and the first match was played on May 14, 1870, at the Botanical Reserve.

THINGS TO DO   The **Nelson Provincial Museum** deals mainly in local history, it's located in Stoke behind **Isel House**, an old homestead built in 1848. The gardens surrounding Isel House include trees from all over the world, many dating back around 100 years.

The **Suter Art Gallery**, next to the Queen's Gardens on Bridge St. has a small but worthwhile collection. Some of the local coffee houses double as galleries, showing works of local artists — of which there are many. In fact, Nelson is known as an arts and crafts-type community. The local clays drew potters to the area and the sea beckoned the artists. **Cottage industries** are plentiful — the PRO can give you a list of artists and craftspeople that welcome visitors.

Christ Church Cathedral, set on a hill and surrounded by gardens, overlooks the downtown Nelson area. Construction of the present Cathedral began in 1925, and after many setbacks and alterations it was completed in the 1960s.

If you've never seen a cob house (the exterior walls are made of earth) you might want to stop by **Broadgreen** on Nayland Rd. in Stoke. It was built in 1855 and modelled after a Devonshire farmhouse.

The **beach** at Tahunanui, 5km south of the city, is safe and popular. Along the shore a recreational area has a roller skating rink, tennis courts, a model boat pond, and Natureland, a small zoo.

PLACES TO STAY   The nearest YHA hostel is 76km away in Havelock. But don't despair, the **Tahuna Beach Holiday Camp** in Tahunanui is the largest motor camp in New Zealand. It's near the beach and the only camp around Nelson on a busline. Go 5km south of the city, ph. 85-158. Campsites are $2.90 for two and cabins are from $4 for two.

The **Brook Reservoir Camp** is also 5km from the city, located in the Brook Valley, ph. 80-399. Tent sites are $2.50 for two and cabins start at $4.10. The **Matai Reserve Motor Camp** is only open during the summer. It's located in the Matai Valley on the river, 6km out. Tent sites are $2.50 for two people.

As far as B&Bs are concerned — the **Seafield Guest House** is at 36 Grove St., ph. 83-502, and charges $9. The **Queen's Garden Guest House**, 342 Hardy St., ph. 88-990, only charges $8.

FOOD   **The Settlers** at 18 Nile St. (across from the Rutherford Hotel) has natural foods, vegetarian dishes, salads, and baked goods to take away or eat there. The prices are reasonable and the food is really good. **Chez Eelco Coffee House** at 296 Trafalgar St. is popular with the locals. The **Hitching Post** is a pizza place located at 145 Bridge St.

ENTERTAINMENT   The **Jet Set Lounge** in the Rutherford Hotel features pop/rock music and dancing nightly for about $2 cover.

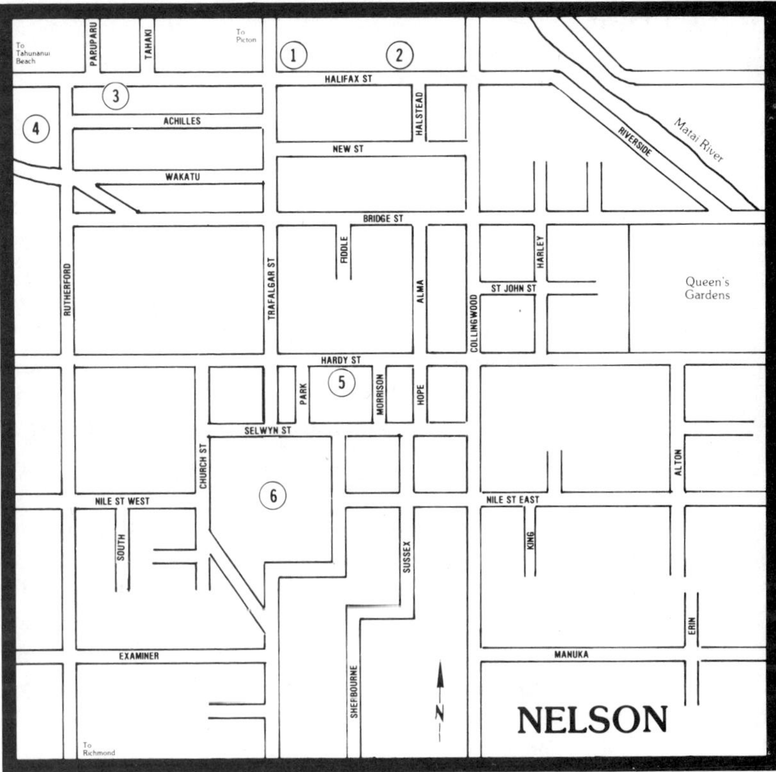

1. PRO
2. AA Office
3. Chief Post Office
4. Anzac Park
5. Newman's
6. Christ Church Cathedral

Golden Bay

Golden Bay is a popular vacation spot with terrific beaches, and it's also the home of Abel Tasman National Park. Takaka is the population center — 900. From Nelson to Takaka you pass through fertile valleys where an abundance of fruit, tobacco, and hops are grown. Then it's over the "marble mountain," the source of Takaka Marble.

The discovery of gold near Collingwood caused the name change to Golden Bay. Tasman had named it Murderer's Bay after four of his crewmen were killed in a Maori ambush when he stopped here in 1642.

The gold finds were patchy and mainly on the surface of river beds, so it wasn't long before it was played out. Most of the prospectors left during the 1860s for the rush of the West Coast and Central Otago.

Farewell Spit is a 35km sandbar which partially shelters Golden Bay from the Tasman Sea. **Cape Farewell**, near the western-most part of the Spit, is the most northern point on the South Island. Collingwood Motors (ph. Collingwood 15S) has excursions to the Spit in 4-wheel drive vehicles. (Motorists are advised not to try and make the trip due to tides and shifting sand.)

The **Pupu Springs** are among the world's largest — over 2 billion liters daily. The whole name is Waikoropupu, which means "bubbling water." In the Anatoki River you can watch tame eels being fed. Go 5km south of Takaka and follow the signs to **Anatoki Eels**. They hibernate from May to August, so don't go then.

Collingwood, 28km northwest of Takaka, is considered a jump-off point for the famous **Heaphy Track**. It's a quiet little town of about 175 people. The **Collingwood Motor Camp** has tent sites for $1 per person, and cabins from $3 for two. Transportation from Collingwood to the head of the Heaphy Track can be arranged through Collingwood Motors.

Since Golden Bay is a popular resort area there are a fair number of motels around. For cheaper rates, however, stick to the motor camps (there is no hostel). The **Pohara Beach Domain Camp** is 10km from Takaka, right on the beach, ph. 59-500. Tent sites are only $3 for two, and cabins start at $7. The **Tukura Motor Camp** is 18km north

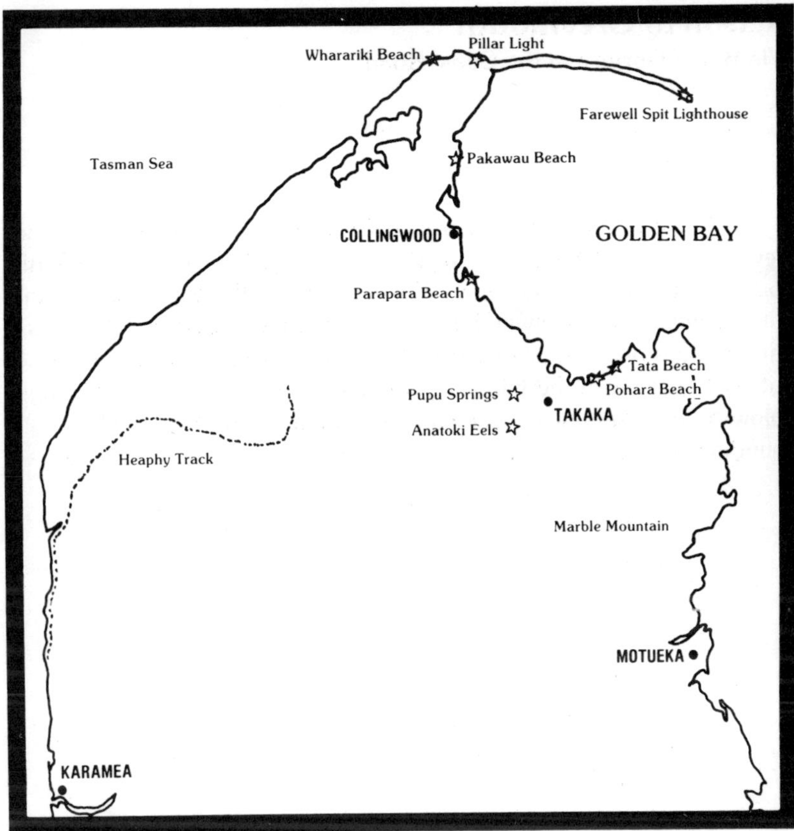

of Takaka, ph. 59-742. Tent sites are $1.50 per person, there are no cabins, but they do have some caravans for hire.

Your best bet for food is in Takaka at the **Wholemeal Trading Co**. It's a health food store and restaurant serving everything from meals to salads, munchies, and omelettes, and they have fantastic fresh fruit milkshakes and sundaes — all at reasonable prices.

Nelson to Greymouth
(Via Buller Gorge and the Coast Road)

The Coast Road from Westport to Greymouth is outstanding — the views of the ocean crashing against the rugged coastline are worth going a little out of your way. Make a stop at the **Punakaiki (Pancake) Rocks** about halfway between Westport and Greymouth. These natural limestone formations look like huge stacks of pancakes rising out of the ocean. If the tide is right you'll see water forced up through **"blow-holes"** (somewhat like geysers erupting) accompanied by resounding booms.

GREYMOUTH

Population: 8,000. Information: PRO — 66 Mawhera Quay, ph. 5101.

Greymouth is the largest city on the West Coast. It got its start during the gold rush of the 1860s, then after the gold was depleted, coal took over as the main industry. Now lumber is the number one commodity of the area — agricultural pursuits are number two.

THINGS TO DO   **Shantytown** is the main attraction around here (go 8km south, turn left at Paroa, continue for 3km). This reconstructed gold town has shops filled with relics — blacksmith, newspaper, bank, grocery, etc. There are stagecoach and hansom cab rides, a steam locomotive ride, or you can pan for gold — color guaranteed. It's open daily, $1.20 admission.

The **Wildlife Park** is on the road to Shantytown (after you turn at Paroa). The wild game here includes chamois, red deer, eels, and wild pigs.

Visits to the **Strongman Coal Mine** can be arranged through the Public Relations Office. The guided tour includes a look at the underground operation.

PLACES TO STAY   The **YHA hostel** is off Cowper St., 1km from the center, ph. 7015.

The **Greymouth Seaside Motor Camp** on Chesterfield St., ph. 6618, is 2km from town, adjacent to the beach (sorry folks, no sand on the beach — just rocks!) Tent sites are $3 for two people, and their cabins start at $5 for two.

The **Golden Coast Guest House** has B&B for $9. It's at 10 Smith St., ph. 7839.

FOOD   Your best bet here is to cook your own or try the pub food — no guarantees!

ENTERTAINMENT   The **Australasian** is popular — then again, all the pubs here seem to do a booming business.

We arrived in Greymouth late in the day, but luckily it was Friday and Friday is late night. After finishing our shopping, we threaded our way through the teenagers toward "home." (They were roaming all over town, aimlessly looking for "action." The policemen followed them, trying to make sure they didn't find any!) Being thirstier than we were hungry, we stopped for a tall, cool one before heading back to cook dinner.

The group at the next table heard our accents and asked us to join them — which led to another jug and another, etc. That was the night we found out that West Coast pubs close when they want to, not when the law says they must. (They usually close when the last drinker leaves!) When we stumbled out at 11:30 to have our belated dinner, the place was still crowded and the party was going strong!

Greymouth to Franz Josef

Hokatika, 45½km south of Greymouth is famous for its greenstone. Two factories in town allow spectators to watch their operations — **Westland Greenstone Co.** on Tancred St. and **Hokatika Jade** on Revell St. Hokatika Jade is also the home of the **Nicholson Boulder**, which contains the largest quantity of gem quality jade ever found in New Zealand — 3720 kilos (over 8000 pounds!)

This section of the Coast Road has some interesting bridges. Not only are they one way — the railroad shares them with cars! (Trains **always** have the right of way — unless you want to argue with a train).

FRANZ JOSEF GLACIER

Population: 400. Information: Westland National Park Headquarters.

The first European to explore the glaciers on the West Coast was Julius von Haast — he named the shorter, steeper one after his Austrian emperor, Franz Josef.

Because of the high amount of rainfall on this portion of the West Coast (over 200 inches annually) there is no "best" time of year to visit and count on fair weather. Even if the morning is fine, there's always a good possibility of clouds obscuring the peaks by mid-day, and then clearing again in the afternoon.

A glacier is created by pressure — when snow crystals are compacted tighter and tighter they form ice. Then the increased pressure caused by more and more snow and ice causes the "river of ice" to flow. (A glacier has to be about 130 ft. (40m) thick before enough pressure is exerted to start the flowing process.)

As climatic conditions change seasonally and vary generally the glacier advances and recedes. At this time glaciers are mostly receding, worldwide. About 14,000 years ago both the Franz Josef and the Fox extended all the way to the coastline.

THINGS TO DO   Obviously the reason most people stop here is to see the glacier — so do it. Here at Franz Josef you can drive 6½km from the main road to the carpark, then walk a short way over a track to the ice.

Inexperienced climbers are advised not to walk onto the glacier without a guide. **Guided glacier walks** (usually twice daily, 9:30 and 1:30) can take care of this problem. An experienced guide will show you around, and you're even provided with any gear which you might need like boots and socks, and walking sticks. Arrangements can be made at the Franz Josef Hotel.

A terrific adventure that is unique to this area is taking a **ski plane flight** (about $30 or $40). Mount Cook Airlines operates this "flightseeing" service from both glaciers, as well as from the Hermitage at Mount Cook. Depending on the length of the flight and the weather conditions you may make a ski-landing on either the Franz Josef, Fox, or Tasman Glacier — a once in a lifetime experience!

There are walks of all types, and leaflets that explain the terrain are available at the park headquarters (as well as lots of other good information).

St. James Anglican Church was built in 1931, with a window behind the altar that originally framed a beautiful view of the glacial ice.

PLACES TO STAY The nearest YHA hostel is at Okarito (pop. 25) 28km north of Franz Josef. It's only a shelter hostel — no electricity.

The **Franz Josef Motor Camp** is ¼ mile south of the township, ph. 826. Tent sites are $1.50 per person (pick a site on high ground in case of rain) and cabins start at $2.50 per bed.

FOOD The **Glacier Restaurant** serves light meals and grills, also has a good variety of baked goods. The **Glacier Store and Tearoom** can provide light meals, plus groceries. The motor camp also has a limited supply of groceries.

ENTERTAINMENT The pub is at the **Franz Josef Hotel**, about ½km north of the township. The **park headquarters** often has an evening program for visitors, the slide shows and talks about the glaciers and surrounding countryside are usually quite good. **Nature walks** are frequently conducted during the day, especially during holidays.

Opossums were introduced during the 19th century to establish a fur industry. They were so prolific that control measures are necessary to keep them from completely overrunning the countryside.

FOX GLACIER

Population: 500. Information: Westland National Park Information Office.

See the chapter on Franz Josef Glacier for a little info about glaciers and how they're formed. Fox is the longer of the two West Coast glaciers, 13½km.

THINGS TO DO You can drive in a little over 5km, then walk the rest of the way to Fox Glacier. **Alpine Guides Ltd.** will provide you with equipment, transportation, and an experienced guide if necessary — half day tours are $4 and full day tours are $9 (bring your own lunch).

As at Franz Josef, there are **airplane flights**, and also **helicopter flights** priced from about $15. If the weather is decent it could be the best $15 you spend in New Zealand — it's that good!

Find out about the numerous walks, and take in slide shows, films, and talks at the park visitor's center. At the center you can also find out more about the **seal colony** at Gillespies Beach, 18km from the township and a **glowworm grotto** just south of town.

PLACES TO STAY The **Fox Glacier Motor Camp**, ph. 821, is just south of town. Tent sites are $3.50 for two people and cabins start from $6 for two. Try not to arrive between 10 a.m. and 2 p.m. because they're closed for cleaning during those hours (and they're not very flexible about it, either!)

FOOD The tea room in town serves light meals and takeaways. The grocery next door is your best bet, though, the selection is better and prices are lower than at the motor camp store.

Over the Haast

Construction of the Haast Pass road was completed in 1960, finally linking the West Coast with the areas further south. It was the original route that the Maoris used to take when they traveled to the Hokatika area for greenstone. The Haast is the lowest pass through the Southern Alps, and although much of the road is unsealed, it's kept in good repair.

There is excellent **fly fishing** for trout near Makarora, check with the ranger station there for details.

WANAKA

Population: 1200. Information: Information Office, Helwitch St., ph. 860 or 660, or the Mount Aspiring National Park Headquarters, Ballantyne Rd. & Main Rd.

After the rain of the West Coast, Wanaka's sunshine is a welcome change — and there's lots of it. That's one of the reasons the area is popular, another is Lake Wanaka. Water sports take precedence here — lots of good fishing, water skiing, and swimming. The town itself is on the southern shore, commanding a magnificent view of the Southern Alps to the north.

THINGS TO DO The walks to **Mount Iron** (1¼ hr. return) and **Mount Roy** (5 hr. return) are popular because they are both such good viewpoints.

Lake Wanaka, with the snow-capped Southern Alps in the background.

The **Wanaka Maze**, ¾ mile from town, is open 7 days, and includes mini-golf, crazy croquet, the maze itself, and New Zealand's largest puzzle shop. The life-size, walk-through maze usually takes about 20 minutes to negotiate, but don't feel like the Lone Ranger if you take 40!

Clutha River Raft Cruises include beautiful scenery — 3½ hr. worth for $6. Other outdoor activities include horseback riding, boat rentals, launch trips, scenic airplane rides, golf, shooting, tramping, and white water canoeing. Stop at the information office to make bookings and get details.

The **Treble Cone Ski Field** is only 29km from Wanaka on the Glendhu Bay Rd. The facilities are growing and becoming quite popular because it's not as crowded as Coronet Peak at Queenstown.

PLACES TO STAY   The **YHA hostel** is at 181 Upton St., ph. 405.

The **Wanaka Islands Domain Camp** is the closest motor camp to town, 1km from the p.o., on Brownston St., ph. 883. The tent sites are $3 for two and cabins are from $6 for two. The **Pleasant Lodge Caravan Park**, 3km out on Glendhu Bay Rd., ph. 207, has tent sites for $3 for two people, but no cabins. The **Penrith Camp** at Beacon Point overlooks the lake, it's also 3km from town, ph. 648. Their tent sites are $2.50 for two people, cabins start at $4.50.

FOOD The **THC Wanaka Hotel** has bistro meals from 6 p.m. to 9 p.m. Monday through Saturday in their family bar. The prices range from $2.25 to $3 for the fully served dinner — including meat, chips and salad. (Good value!)

QUEENSTOWN

Population: 3,000. Information: PRO — Camp St., GTO — Beach St., Mount Cook Travel — The Mall and Rees St., or H & H Tour Bookings — Shotover St. The information offices are all open every day.

Plan on budgeting a little extra money for Queenstown. It's not that prices are high — there's just so much more to do, and everything does have its price. Queenstown is **the** resort area of the South Island. In the summer people flock to the shores of beautiful Lake Wakatipu for a little fun in the sun, and in the winter they come from all over to ski at New Zealand's most famous ski field, Coronet Peak. The town fills up to overflowing around Christmas, but the friendly atmosphere and comradery make up for any inconveniences. Just be sure to book ahead for lodgings and the more popular attractions so you won't be disappointed.

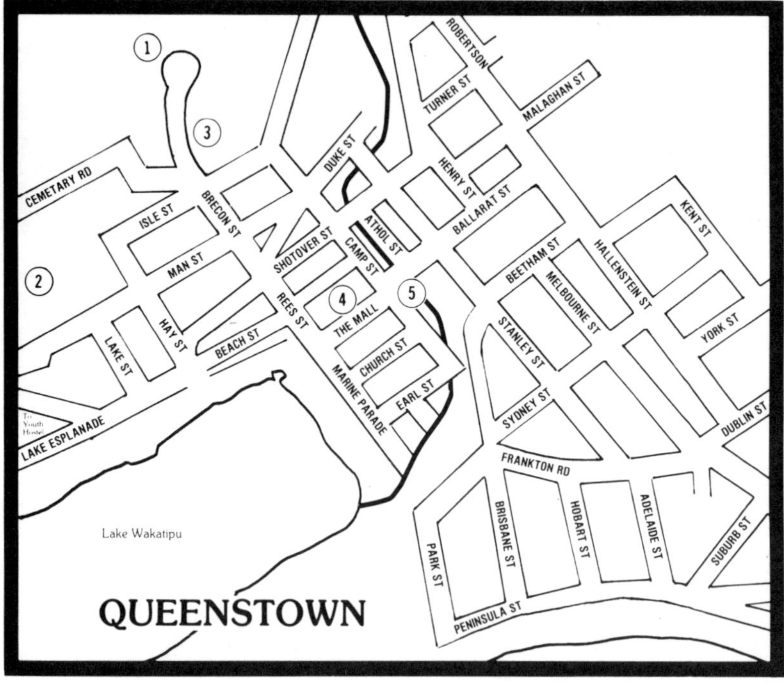

The largest gold rush in New Zealand history started here in 1862. The main workings were in the Arrow River, but William Rees' station became the center of commerce for the area, and Queenstown grew from there. As more and more men arrived, they went further to stake claims — on the Shotover, Stoney Creek, and at Skippers.

Lake Wakatipu is the second largest of the South Island's many lakes (Te Anau is the largest).

A trip to **Arrowtown**, 20km to the northeast, gives an idea of the way things were during the gold rush. The museum there has an excellent display on gold mining.

THINGS TO DO There are at least ten different boat trips available, from **lake cruises** on the T.S.S. Earnslaw, a vintage steamer ($3.50 to $6.50) to wild **white water rafting** on the Shotover's Lower Gorge (Kon Tiki Rafts, $33). In between the extremes — catamaran sailing ($10 per hour), leisurely **raft trips** on the Shotover ($6), **jet boat trips** ($8 to $12), a **hydrofoil trip** on the lake ($8), or many others. Any of the booking agencies can help you choose and make arrangements.

Fishing charters are available from $16 per hour for two people, and Queenstown Sports on Rees St. has lots of information on where to catch fish if you're on your own, as well as a full line of supplies that you might need.

If you haven't seen any sheep dogs in action yet, trips to the **Walter Peak Station** include a brief but informative session with sheep dogs. It's great to see how much they enjoy their work.

To get a good view of the area you can take the **gondola ride** up to the Skyline Chalet ($2.50). Or go out to **Deer Park Heights**, a game reserve overlooking the lake and Queenstown. If you have a car (the only way to get there) the view is worth the trip, and the deer, chamois, wapiti, and mountain goats just enhance it. Also in the livestock line, at the **Cattledrome**, $1.50, you can milk a cow, or if you just want to look at animals try the **zoo** at Frankton (60¢).

---

1. Gondola Terminal	4. PRO
2. Motor Camp	5. Post Office
3. Motor Museum	6. GTO

Gold Terrace Mining Town is a recreated gold rush village ($1.50) and the **Motor Museum** is also of historic value. There are over 60 exhibits, from a 1922 Rolls Royce to an airplane ($1.50). The **Sight and Sound Show** depicts what it was like in Queenstown during the gold rush days ($1.50).

You can also go **flightseeing by helicopter** (from $9.50) or take a trip to Milford Sound the quick way — an hour and fifteen minutes return by airplane (from $35).

Go **horseback riding** and catch some views for $7.50, take a 4-wheel drive trip to **Moke Lake** ($10.50), or go on a bus trip (**Coronet Peak**, $6, or **Skipper's Canyon**, $7.50). **Dane's Back Country Experiences** has trips from two hours to twelve days — for the adventurer.

Queenstown is also a jump-off point for the **Routeburn Track**, see the walking track chapter for details or stop by H&H Bookings. The **Fur 'n Wood** on Beach St. rents bicycles, golf clubs, sleeping bags, tents, etc. for the unprepared (or light) traveler.

PLACES TO STAY   There's a **YHA hostel** across from the lake on Lake Esplanade, ph. 352. **Hunter House** on Man St. isn't a hostel, but they have shared rooms for $23 a week.

The **Queenstown Motor Park** is 1km from town, ph. 164. Tent sites are $2.75 for two people, with cabins from $7 for two — book ahead. The **Frankton Motor Camp** is 6km from town on the Frankton arm of Lake Wakatipu, ph. 247. Tent sites are $2.50 for two people, cabins start at $5 for two.

The **Mountain View Lodge Caravan Park** is 1km out on Frankton Rd. overlooking the lake, ph. 153. Tent sites are $3 for two and cabins start at $8. And last but not least, the **Queenstown Holiday Park** is 4km from town at Arthur's Point, ph. 1180. Tent sites for two people are $3 and cabins are from $7.

Both of these bed and breakfasts charge $9: **Melbourne House**, on Melbourne St., ph. 378, and the **Goldfields Guest House** at 41 Frankton Rd., ph. 221M.

Some of the motels in the area are pretty inexpensive (for motels). The **Melbourne House** on Melbourne St., ph. 378, is from $17.50 for two. The **Mountain View Lodge** on Frankton Rd., ph. 153, is $8 per person, and the **Aroha Motel** at 20 Hay St., ph. 1017, is $16 for two.

FOOD   Try the **Loaf-In Bakery** in the Rees Place Arcade for fresh bread (and pastries!). **Cadrona's**, on the Mall, has pancakes, breakfasts, and lunches, but they close early. **Down to Earth** at 5 Beach St., has wholemeal goodies, salads, and sandwiches (take away only). **Saguero's**, on the Mall, is more expensive, but they have Mexican food! It's really good, and priced from $2 to $4, lunch or dinner, BYO.

The **Cow Pizza and Spaghetti House** in Cow Lane (between BNZ and National Bank on Rees St.) costs a bit, too. But the pizza is really good and they have a full Italian menu. If you really want to do it up — try **Upstairs, Downstairs** or the **Continental**, both in the Mall.

ENTERTAINMENT   Queenstown has nightlife! It's really hot during the ski season, but compared to the rest of the country it's even great during the summer. **O'Connell's Hotel** has a smorgasbord and live entertainment at least three nights a week, for $3. The **Diggins Bar** on Beach St. often has someone playing guitar, it's usually a busy place.

But the "deal" is at the **Skyline Chalet**, when they have a "Swinger's Night" on Tuesday, Thursday, and Sunday from 6:30 to 12:30. The $7 admission fee includes the gondola ride, a great smorgasbord, and dancing to pop/rock music until 12:30.

TE ANAU

Population: 2,000. Information: Fiordland Travel — Te Anau Tce. & Milford Rd., ph. 859, Mount Cook Travel — Te Anau Tce., ph. 494, or Fiordland National Park Headquarters, Te Anau Tce.

The tiny town of Te Anau is considered by most to be the jumping off point for the famous Milford Track. This is where the people on the guided walk sleep in their last real bed and eat in their last restaurant before they "hit the wilderness" for five days.

Te Anau is a nice town — relaxing. Swim, go boating, fish, take a guided excursion, but above all discover Fiordland at your own pace and enjoy.

THINGS TO DO The **Te Ana-au Caves** are a major attraction. The two-hour launch trip takes you through the "cave of rushing waters" where you'll see waterfalls, limestone formations, and a glowworm grotto, all for $6.50. Other half and full day **launch trips** on Lakes Te Anau and Manapouri have destinations like Glade House (the start of the Milford walk), Stockyard Cove, Deep Cove, and Doubtful Sound, from $5 to $27. The Deep Cove and Doubtful Sound trips both include a tour of the **Manapouri Hydro-electric Power Station**, which is located underground.

Scenic flights by float plane or land-based aircraft range from 10 minutes to over an hour, with itineraries like the hidden lakes, highlights of Fiordland, and Milford Sound ($10 to $35). **Coach tours** leave for Milford daily at 8:15 and return around 6:00, $10. Or you can take a bus one way and fly the other for about $30.

If you like fish, but not fishing, go to the **Underground Trout Observatory** across from the park headquarters. For 50ᶜ you can look at rainbow and brown trout for as long as you like. There's a **Wapiti Park** 5km down the road to Manapouri that has wapiti, deer, chamois, and tahr, or go see the **Wildlife Museum** on Milford Rd. for displays of all types of New Zealand birds and animals — but they're all stuffed.

For a little more action — **fishing and hunting charters** can be arranged, or rent a boat. **River trips** on the Waiau by jet boat or raft cost from $5.50 to $10, and at **Lil' Golf** you can play miniature golf or rent a bicycle.

PLACES TO STAY The **YHA hostel** is 1½km from town on the Milford Rd., no phone.

The **Mountain View Cabins and Caravan Park** is only ½km from the center, ph. 644. There are no tent sites, but they have cabins from $6.50 for two. The **Te Anau Motor Camp** is 1km from town, ph. 646. Tent sites are $1.40 per person and cabins start at $6.50 for two. They also have **dormitory** accommodations (men's, women's, and mixed) for $3 per person.

The **Matai Lodge** at Matai and Mokonui Sts., ph. 818, is a good B&B for two, the regular $10.50 single rate is lowered to $16.50 for two people sharing a room. The **Bluegum Lodge** at 10 Dusky St., ph. 772, is $9.

FOOD The **Takahe Tea Room** on Milford Rd. can satisfy your craving for spicy food — the chili is guaranteed to make your eyes water — it's terrific! They also serve pies, sandwiches, and meals. The only other good bet is the **Grubsteak Restaurant and Family Bar** in the Te Anau Hotel complex. They serve bistro food from $2.50 to $3.25, but the portions are controlled, so don't expect a lot for your money.

ENTERTAINMENT There's a **disco** at the Te Anau Hotel on Fridays and Saturdays from 7:30, $1 cover charge. The Te Anau Hotel also shows current movies, slide shows, and wildlife presentations a few nights a week.

MILFORD SOUND

After a glacier melts, it leaves a trough in the land. When the sea enters this trough the resulting waterway is called a fiord — and Milford Sound is one of New Zealand's most spectacular Fiords. The glacial action cut almost 1200m straight into the earth, and now these vertical walls enclose the sound.

A Scot sealer named Donald Sutherland was the first person to live at Milford. After his discovery of 580m high **Sutherland Falls**, he realized the potential of the area and built the first hotel at Milford City.

THINGS TO DO Nearly everything at Milford revolves around sightseeing on the sound . . . and rightfully so. **Scenic flights** by Mount Cook Airlines run from 10 to 40 minutes, cost from $8 to $25. You can include a little scenery or a lot — Mitre Peak, the entrance to the fiord, Sutherland Falls, mountains, lakes, glaciers, and even the Milford Track.

The most popular thing to do at Milford is to take a **launch trip** on the fiord. You can choose a one or two-hour trip, the longer one goes all the way to the Tasman Sea.

PLACES TO STAY There's not much of a choice here — the THC Hotel and the hostel are all there is. The **hostel** is also run by the THC, cost is about $5 per person, depending on the type of facilities you require.

FOOD Bring your own if you can, but don't plan to cook it at the hostel (no cooking facilities!) There's a **smorgasbord lunch** at the hotel for about $5 that's a good deal if you can get by on one meal per day.

INVERCARGILL

Population: 52,000. Information: PRO — 40 Don St., ph. 84-538 or GTO — Esk St. (off Dee St.)

Invercargill's economy is based on grass — the kind that sheep eat. The city is surrounded by freezing works and nearly 7 million animals are killed each year. The rainfall here is spread evenly throughout the year, which accounts for the beautiful green fields that the sheep and cattle love to eat. And because the area is relatively flat the farmers can graze more animals per acre than many other places.

Invercargill instituted the licensing trust concept of liquor sales in 1943. For many years the city had been "dry" and in order to make money and keep control, the decision was made for the city council to operate the liquor licenses. Many other cities have followed the example — the trust has accumulated over $25 million in assets since the system's beginning.

THINGS TO DO The **Southland Centennial Museum and Art Gallery** near the entrance to Queens Park on Gala St. is a good provincial museum. It's the only place in New Zealand that **tuataras** can be seen in their simulated native habitat. These lizards grow to about 60cm and are the only survivors of the same prehistoric order that included dinosaurs — they're often called "living fossils."

Queens Park consists of 80 hectares in downtown Invercargill. There is a deer park, an aviary, and beautiful flower gardens. **Anderson Park** is 7km north of the city. It's the historic home of Sir Robert Anderson, an early businessman of Southland, and houses the **City Art Gallery.**

If you're not planning to spend some time on **Stewart Island**, at least take a day excursion. If you take the ferry, it costs $10 (when you return the same day) and you spend about four hours on the island. There are also airplane flights across Foveaux Strait, they're costlier.

PLACES TO STAY There's a **YHA hostel** at 122 North Rd., about

2km from the p.o., ph. 59-344.

The **Southland A&P Assn. Caravan Park** is 1km from the p.o. on Victoria Ave. (off Dee St.) ph. 88-787. Tent sites are $2 a night for two persons, and cabins start at $6. The **Raceway Caravan Park** is at 705 Tay St., ph. 76-046. Tent sites cost $3.50 a night for two, cabins from $7. The **Beach Road Motor Camp** is on the road to Oreti Beach (8km from the p.o., 1km from the beach) ph. 84-408. Tent sites here are $2 for two and the cabins start at $5.

The **Apollo House Private Hotel** at 8 Compton St., ph. 66-063, has B&B for $9.50.

FOOD   The **Food Factory** on Dee St. makes excellent pizza, it's open 7 days.

1. Motor Camp	3. Railway Station
2. Automobile Assn.	4. Chief Post Office

To
Lumsden
HERBERT ST
KING ST
INVERCARGILL
Queen's
Park
QUEENS DRIVE
SYDNEY ST
ST ANDREW ST
1
GALA ST
YARROW ST
2
DEE ST
KELVIN ST
JED ST
MARY ST
LINDISFARNE ST
To
Dunedin
DON ST
3
TAY ST
4
TYNE ST
To
Oreti
Beach
TWEED ST
CLYDE ST
NINTH ST
YTHAM ST
PRINCES ST
NELSON ST
POMONA ST
MORTON ST
BIGGAR ST
To Bluff

Stewart Island

Stewart Island's Maori name is Rakiura, which means "heavenly glow." The name has been attributed to the beautiful sunrises and sunsets, and perhaps the Southern Lights, the aurora australis.

The trip across Foveaux Strait can be made in two ways — by

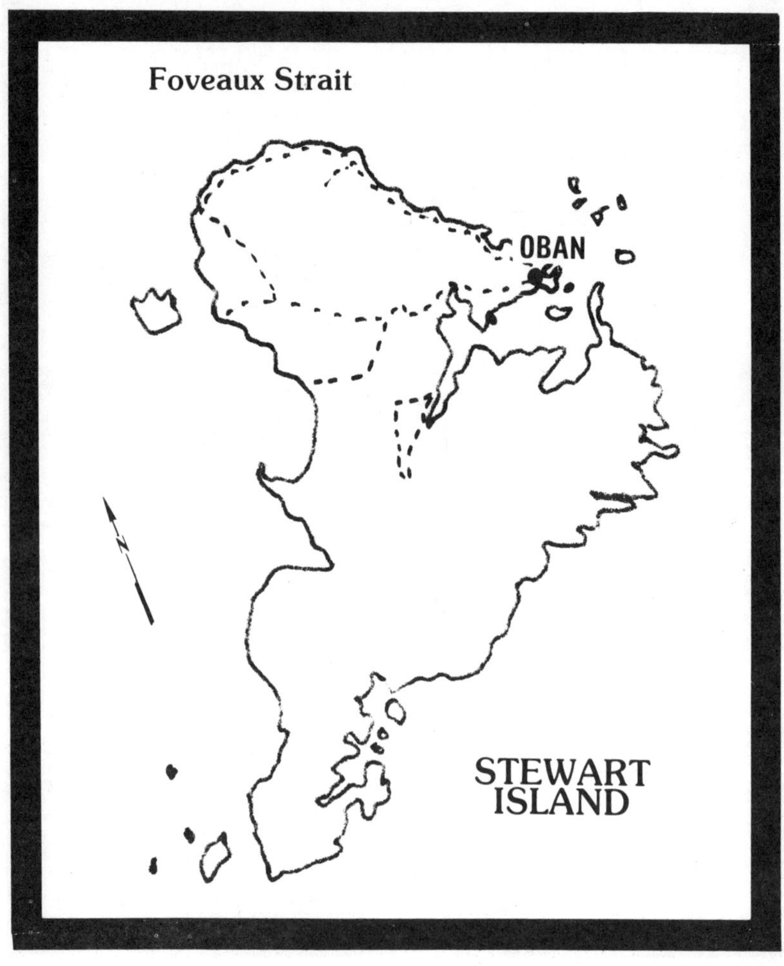

airplane or ferry. The ferry crosses from Bluff, taking about two hours. The day excursion costs $10, and you spend about four hours on the island before the return trip. If you're staying longer than one day the ferry ride is $12 return. The airplane is obviously more expensive, but it only takes 20 minutes and leaves from the Invercargill airport, so it's more convenient.

When the Maoris sold Stewart Island to the pakehas they kept all rights to the Muttonbird Islands off the coast. These islands are the breeding grounds for the New Zealand muttonbird, which is used as a source of oil and feather down. They are also eaten, and taste somewhat like mutton (makes sense, doesn't it?)

Stewart Island was first a port for sealers, then whalers. About 1860 sawmills made their debut — they lasted 60 years, then the government decided not to renew timber rights, feeling that the island was better suited to being a reserve. There was a little tin and gold mining before the turn of the century, and today the people here make their living from the sea.

Stewart Island is a haven for the back-to-nature crowd. Almost all the activities here are related to the outdoors — tramping, walking, swimming, fishing, and launch trips. The forest service office in Oban can provide details about tracks and huts. Hunting permits are available there also. Stewart Island is the home of the last accessible herd of **white tail (Virginia) deer** in New Zealand. The larger red deer can also be hunted.

As far as accommodations go — there's a hotel and a few motels in Oban, all in the $20 range. A good place to camp is at **Horseshoe Haven**, 4km from Half Moon Bay at Horseshoe Bay. It costs about $2 a person. They also have a few cabins for $11 for two people. Otherwise you can camp in the bush or on one of the many beaches around the coast — there's lots of island, but very few people.

DUNEDIN

Population: 115,000. Information: PRO — 119 Princes St., ph. 76-765 or GTO — 123 Princes St., ph. 40-349. (Both offices are only about two blocks from the Octagon, which is considered the center of the city.)

Dunedin is a university town — that means there's almost always something going on, from rock concerts to lectures and theatrical productions. Plan to spend a few extra days here enjoying the city's restaurants, movies, and pubs with bands, without the "big city" atmosphere you might expect. You can even catch some sun and surf out at the beaches!

A man named Frederick Tucket chose the site for Dunedin — it was to be a Scottish settlement. Even today, many things around the area have a Scottish flavor, especially the name, which means New Edinburgh. In 1844 Tucket paid the three local Maori chiefs 2400 pounds for 162,000 hectares of land. It was quite a bargain — that works out to about a penny per acre!

The gold rush of 1861 gave Dunedin its real start. Ships passing through the port strengthened the economy, and the building of many large Victorian structures gave the town a look of permanence. Dunedin was the largest city in New Zealand during this period.

Dunedin's cable car system (necessary to conquer all those hills) was the second one built in the world (San Francisco built the first). It remained operative for 75 years, until in 1957 the Mornington line was the last to close down. The first university in the country was established in Dunedin — the University of Otago opened in 1869. One other claim to fame — Wilson Distillers Ltd. of Dunedin is the only whiskey distillery in the country.

1. Olveston	5. GTO
2. YWCA	6. PRO
3. Chief Post Office	7. Early Settler's Museum
4. The Exchange	8. Road Services Depot
9. Railway Station	

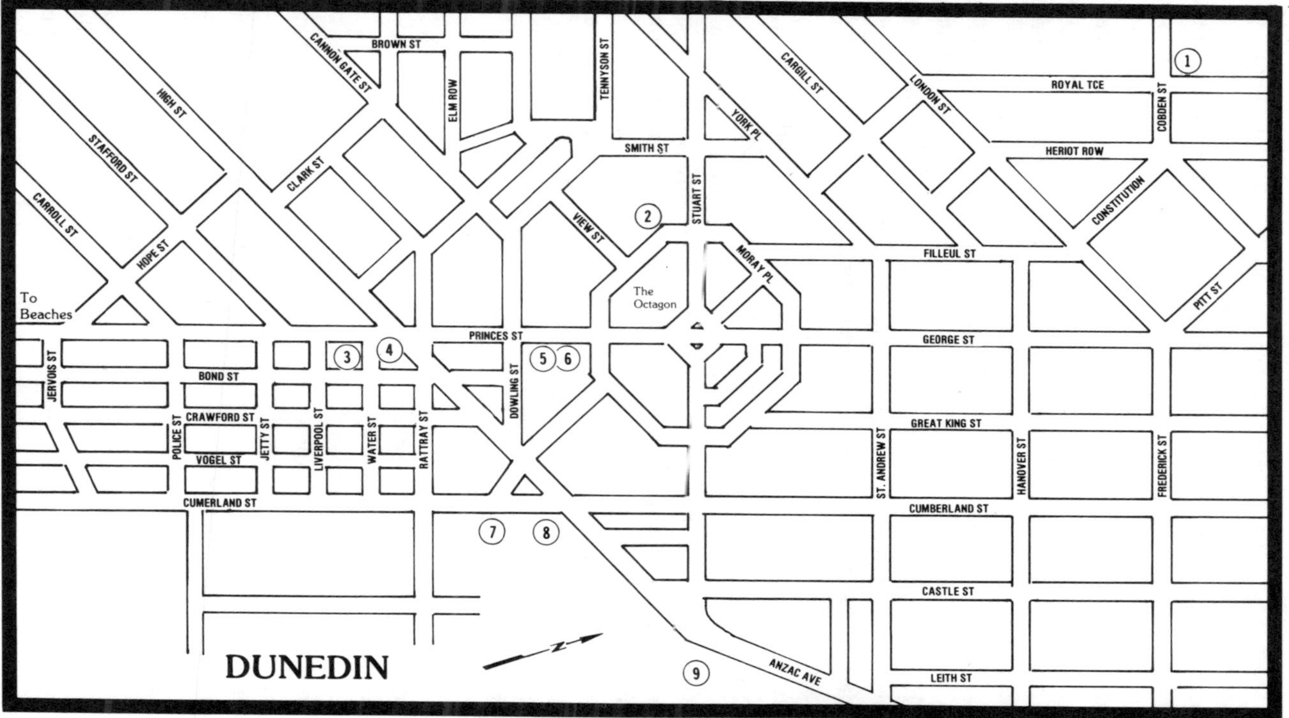
DUNEDIN
The Octagon
To Beaches
1
2
3
4
5
6
7
8
9
HIGH ST
STAFFORD ST
CARROLL ST
HOPE ST
CANNON GATE ST
BROWN ST
ELM ROW
CLARK ST
TENNYSON ST
SMITH ST
VIEW ST
YORK PL
STUART ST
MORAY PL
CARGILL ST
LONDON ST
ROYAL TCE
COBDEN ST
HERIOT ROW
CONSTITUTION
FILLEUL ST
PITT ST
PRINCES ST
DOWLING ST
GEORGE ST
JERVOIS ST
BOND ST
CRAWFORD ST
POLICE ST
VOGEL ST
JETTY ST
LIVERPOOL ST
WATER ST
RATTRAY ST
CUMERLAND ST
GREAT KING ST
ST. ANDREW ST
HANOVER ST
FREDERICK ST
CUMBERLAND ST
CASTLE ST
ANZAC AVE
LEITH ST
N

THINGS TO DO   There are lots of "architectural wonders" (i.e. old buildings) to look at — find out about walking tours of the city at the PRO. One building of note is **Olveston**, at the corner of Royal Terrace and Cobden St. This 35-room Jacobean style mansion is open for public tours. The original furnishings and the garden setting combine to make it a "treasure from the age of gracious living." (And it's a fun way to see how the "other half" used to live!) Guided tours from 9:30 daily, 1:30 on Sunday. Call ahead to reserve a place on the tour of your choice, $1.

If you like beautiful old buildings, **Larnach's Castle**, out on the Otago Peninsula, is a must. It was begun in 1871, and cost about 150,000 pounds (around three million dollars by today's standards!) The ceiling in the foyer alone took three men 6½ years to carve! The present owners, Mr. and Mrs. Barker, are in the process of restoring it to its former magnificence, replacing the furnishings and doing an incredible amount of work to both the Castle and the grounds. Open daily from 9 a.m. to 5 p.m., $2.

Dunedin has two good museums. The **Otago Museum** on Great King St. has a fine collection of art and sculpture, early maps and paintings that show the growth of Dunedin from a farming settlement to a city, and many Maori artifacts — including preserved heads! (Head preserving used to be popular, but fortunately it went out of style over 100 years ago.) The Hocken Library wing has one of the best collections of New Zealand history around.

The **Early Settler's Museum** in Lower High St. includes a large collection of pioneer's portraits. Among the other paraphernalia on display is a really large item — Josephine, one of the first locomotives used in the area.

The **Royal Albatross Colony** near Taiaroa Head is the only place in the world where these huge birds (their wingspan can reach 3m) nest so near civilization. The area is carefully controlled, so reservations are required, and can be made through the GTO. The admission fee is $2.50. If you don't have transportation, the only alternative is a tour bus, daily at 9:15, for $7.50. (It's a long way out to Taiaroa Head!)

There are some other interesting things on the Otago Peninsula besides the Castle and the albatrosses. The **Glenfalloch Woodland Gardens** are famous for the rhododendrons. Peacocks wander through the grounds, and the woodsy setting

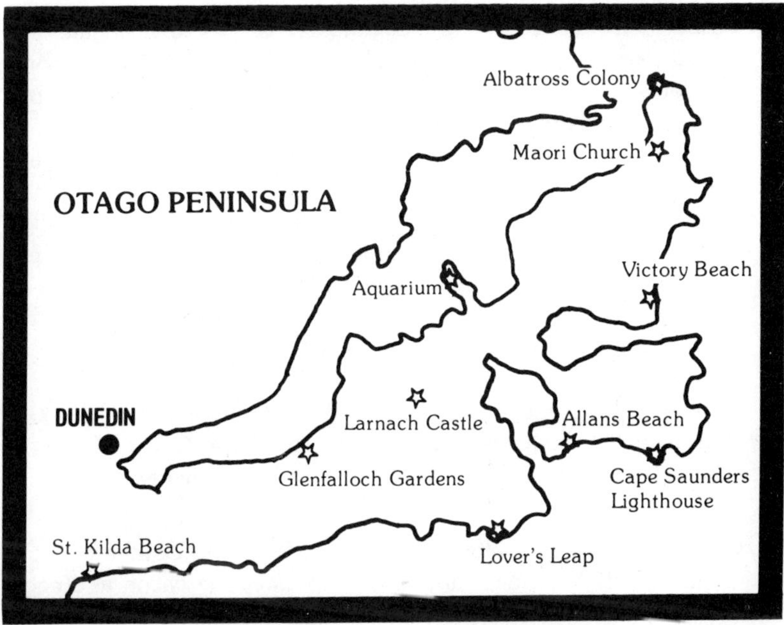

makes a nice picnic spot. The **Portobello Marine Laboratory and Aquarium** is run by the University of Otago, and has displays of all sorts of New Zealand water life. **Seals and sea lions** are often spotted near the **Cape Saunders Lighthouse**, and some famous Maoris are buried at the **Otakou Maori Church**. The church grounds also include a small museum.

The **Dunedin City Tour** was the best city tour we took. It includes points of interest within the city to give you an idea of where things are located, then takes you by the **ocean beaches** of St. Kilda and St. Clair. A tour of Larnach's Castle is followed by a stop at Glenfalloch Gardens. It's particularly good if you don't have your own transportation, because it's the only way to see the castle. The cost is $5.50, and the tour runs daily at 2 p.m. Reservations are a good idea (in the off-season there is a 6 passenger minimum . . . something to do with the taxis).

Factory tours are available — two favorites are the Cadbury Chocolate plant (the smell of chocolate permeates downtown Dunedin), and Schweppes Hudson, a soft drink bottler. The PRO has a list of these and others, including times and necessary arrangements.

PLACES TO STAY The **YHA hostel** is at 412 Highgate St., about 2km from the Octagon, ph. 741-919. The **YWCA** accommodates both women and men, it's in Moray Place, ph. 776-781, $8 B&B.

There are two campgrounds fairly close-in. The **Tahuna Seaside Camp** on Victoria Rd. in St. Kilda is adjacent to the beach. Take a St. Kilda bus from the Exchange (Princes & High Sts.). Tent sites are $3 for two people and cabins start at $2 per person, ph. 54-690. The **Aaron Lodge Motor Camp** is at 176 Kaikorai Valley Rd., ph. 64-725. A Bradford bus from the Octagon will get you there. Tent sites are $2.50 for two, cabins start at $6.

The **Sahara Guest Lodge** at 619 George St., ph. 776-662, has bed and breakfast for $9. The **Excelsior Guest House** at Princes & Dowling Sts., ph. 776-848, is a little higher at $10.

FOOD The **Amigo Coffee Bar**, across from the Southern Cross Hotel on High St. has super pies (especially the bacon and egg). **Barry's Coffee Lounge** on George St. near the Octagon specializes in pancakes — American style includes pancakes, 2 eggs, and ham for only $1.50. At **Potpourri Natural Foods**, 97 Lower Stuart St., you can get wholemeal food, sandwiches, and good salads, and it's all reasonably priced.

The **European Hotel Bistro Bar** serves really good quality meals from $1.80 to $3.50. It's located on George St., one block from the Octagon. And **Big Daddy's**, a takeaway on the Octagon, serves plain old takeaway food — their gimic is that they're open 24 hours a day, every day. (Really unusual for New Zealand!)

ENTERTAINMENT The **Regent Theatre** on the Octagon usually has something going, often programs by internationally-known performers. The **European Hotel's San Fran Disco** is open Tuesday through Saturday, with a cover of $1. And the **Downtown Tavern** on the corner of Princes and Police Sts. has live music Thursday, Friday, and Saturday nights — get there early if you like to sit down between dances!

The kea is an alpine parrot common to the high areas of the South Island. He's mostly a dull olive green, but the feathers on the undersides of the wings are brilliant orangey-red.

MOUNT COOK

Information: Mount Cook National Park Headquarters.

The area around the Hermitage (probably the most famous hotel in New Zealand, part of the THC chain) is the center of activity for Mount Cook National Park. This is where you'll find accommodations, a store, and park headquarters.

Mount Cook (its Maori name is Aorangi, "Cloud in the Sky") at 3762.9m (12,345 ft.) is the tallest peak in New Zealand. It was first scaled by three Kiwis on Christmas Day, 1894, and many from all over the world have climbed it since.

Himalayan tahr, European chamois, and to a lesser extent red deer, all roam the park. Their introduction is regretted, however, because they've been quite prolific and now are causing soil erosion and damage to the vegetation. Shooting of these animals, now considered pests, is encouraged — talk to the people at the park headquarters first.

THINGS TO DO   The bus trip to **Tasman Glacier** is a highlight of many Mount Cook visits. You can hire hiking equipment if necessary for the hike onto the glacier. As at Franz Josef and Fox Glaciers there are **airplane rides** at Mount Cook, from $30 to $40. The scenery is magnificent and landing on a glacier in a ski plane is truly a once in a lifetime experience (unless you already did it on the West Coast!)

There is some **skiing** all year round, but obviously the best is during the winter months. A really unique skiing adventure is the 15-mile trip down Tasman Glacier — enquire at park headquarters.

There are lots of walks, tramps, and climbs within the park, from the 10-minute Bowen Track and its view of Mount Cook to climbing the mountain itself. The **Copland Track** is usually crossed from the Mount Cook side, guides can be hired at **Alpine Guides Ltd.** at the Hermitage. This company also runs a **School of Mountaineering** on set dates — write to P.O. Box 20, Mount Cook.

Remember that park headquarters is the outdoor activity center — at times there are rangers available to accompany groups and individuals on climbs and tramps. If you have any questions about the flora and fauna, the mountains and glaciers, walking tracks, etc., they'll probably be able to help you out.

PLACES TO STAY   The **YHA hostel** is across from park headquarters. Unless you're a YHA member you're out of luck as far as cheap accommodations go. The motel flats start at about $20 for two, the Hermitage costs $30 and up. If you can get a group of five together the **Mount Cook Chalets** are a good deal ($17 for the first two, $2.50 each for the next three, totalling $24.50, or about $5 each).

FOOD   You just have to remember that this is a resort. We strongly recommend bringing your own food or buying it at the store here (although it's a little cheaper to bring your own). The THC complex runs all of the eating places, they seem to forget that we're not all part of the affluent middle class.

CHRISTCHURCH

Population: 300,000 (urban area). Information: PRO — Worcester St. & Oxford Tce., ph. 799-629 or GTO — Cathedral Square, ph. 794-900. Christchurch has a good public transportation system — check the kiosk in Cathedral Square, chances are that a bus goes near where you want to go.

Christchurch is often called "the most English city outside of England." The streets are named after English bishoprics, the Avon River flows placidly through the city, the neo-gothic cathedral dominates the Square, and the older buildings of the city have a definitely medieval air. Many trace their start in New Zealand to the First Four Ships which brought the first colonists to Canterbury in late 1850.

Christchurch is currently a shipping center (through Lyttelton Harbor to the south), a travel center (most Australian flights originate or land at Christchurch International), a sports center, and the largest population center on the South Island.

Operation Deep Freeze, the peaceful exploration of Antarctica, is dependent on Christchurch for supplies and many of the earlier Antarctic expeditions started from this southern city. The Canterbury Museum has a large antarctic exhibit.

THINGS TO DO Christchurch is really flat — a perfect city to explore by bicycle. **Rent-a-Bike** at the Avon Carpark Building, 82 Worcester St., has bikes for hire from 50ᶜ per hour or $3 per day. They're open 7 days.

By picking up the *Official Guide to Christchurch and Canterbury* (published monthly) at the PRO or GTO, you can get a really good idea of what's going on.

Canterbury Museum, at the entrance to the Botanic Gardens on Rolleston Ave., includes exhibits on early New Zealand, Oriental Art, birds, and Antarctica. There is also a **planetarium**. The museum is open daily from 10 a.m. to 4:30, 2 p.m. to 4:30 on Sundays.

The **Ferrymead Historic Park** is in Heathcote (take a Sumner bus from the Square) and it's a "living museum" of transport and technology, open 10 a.m. to 4 p.m. daily. Ferrymead isn't to be confused with the **Yaldhurst Transport Museum**, which also houses displays pertaining to transportation.

The **Willowbank Wildlife Reserve** is Christchurch's "zoo." Located at 60 Hussey Rd., there are camels, monkeys, wallabies, deer, and mountain lions, and over 400 birds among the exhibits. Admission is 80^c. The **Orana Wildlife Park**, Harewood Rd. W. extension, is a drive-through lion reserve ($2). There are also kangaroos, monkeys, etc.

Christchurch Cathedral dominates the Square and the downtown area. If you're lost — just look for the 65½m high spire. For a small fee you can climb to the top of the tower and get a good view of the city.

The **Town Hall** complex is considered the finest conference facility in the country. The fountain in front is featured on many tourist folders, it looks like huge dandelions gone to seed.

The closest **beach** is at New Brighton (9km) where you'll also find **Queen Elizabeth II Park**, which was built for the 1974 Commonwealth Games. New Brighton has **Saturday shopping**, too.

Boating is popular — from **canoeing on the Avon** (rentals from the Antigua Boat Shed, 10 a.m. to 5 p.m.), to **jet boating** on the outlying rivers and **sailing** in Lyttelton Harbor and around Banks Peninsula. Two other **swimming beaches** are at Sumner (12km) and Taylor's Mistake (16km). **Fishing** for lake and river trout gives way during a part of the year for **salmon fishing** in the Rakaia River.

Mt. Hutt is the largest ski field in the area, but there are 10 others nearby. Contact Snowline Sports Center at 250 Oxford Terrace for details.

Bus tours are operated by the Christchurch Transport Board and private companies. See Banks Peninsula, Christchurch by Night, or take the Harbor, City, or Suburban Tours. **White water rafting** and **fishing tours** are available through Alpine River Tours and you can even fly to **Mount Cook** via Mount Cook Airlines ($63).

PLACES TO STAY There are two YHA hostels in Christchurch. The **Cora Wilding Hostel** is 5km from the Square at 9 Evelyn Couzins Ave., ph. 899-199. **Rolleston House** is only two km

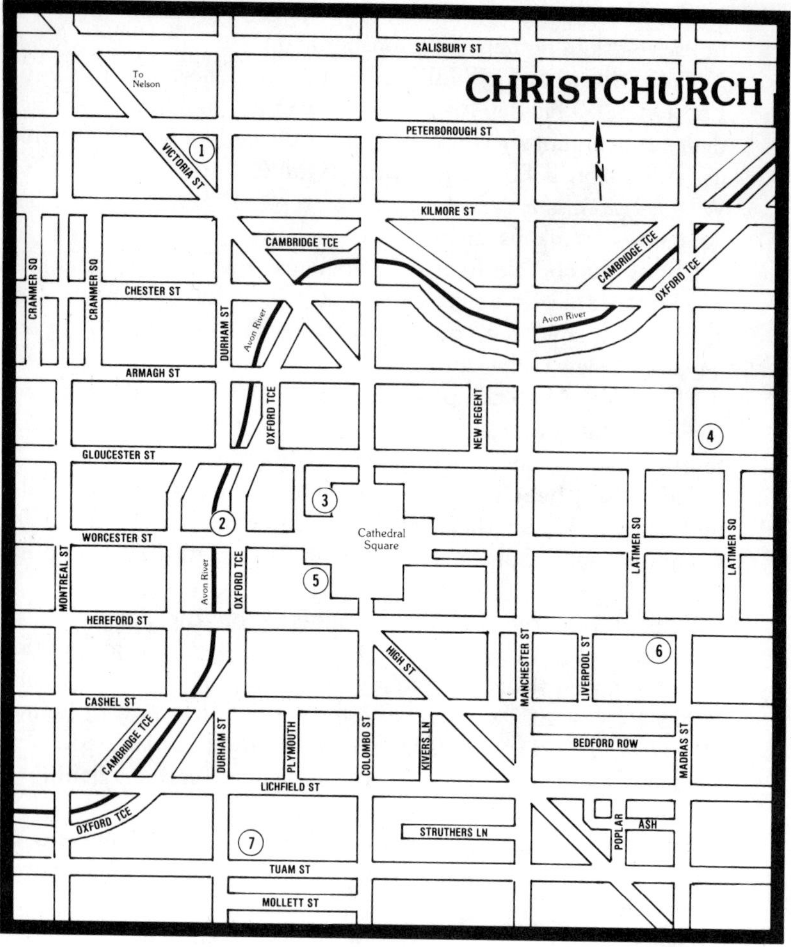

1. Railways Bus Depot
2. PRO
3. GTO
4. YWCA
5. Chief Post Office
6. AA Office
7. Newman's

from the Square at 5 Worcester St.

The **YWCA** has a hostel in Latimer Square, ph. 798-429. They take women and men, $6 B&B or $4 B&B if you use your sleeping bag. The **YMCA** is at 12 Hereford St., ph. 60-689. They also accommodate both men and women, for $6 B&B or $7.50 for dinner, bed, and breakfast.

There are seven motor camps within 10km of the Square. The **Addington Showground Camp** is closest to downtown, 3km from the Square, at 47 Whiteleigh Ave., ph. 389-770. Take a Lincoln Rd. bus. Tent sites are $2 for two and cabins start at $4. The **Meadow Park Motor Camp** is 5km from the Square on Meadow St., off Main North Road, ph. 529-176. Take a Papanui bus. Tent sites are $1.60 per person and cabins are from $7 for two.

The **Riccarton Park Motor Camp** is 6km from the Square on the Main South Road in Upper Riccarton, ph. 45-690. Tent sites are $2.40 for two, cabins from $5. Take a Riccarton bus. The **Russley Park Motor Camp** is opposite the Riccarton Race Course, 6km from the Square, at 372 Yaldhurst Rd., ph. 427-021. Take a Russley Rd. or Fovant St. bus. Tent sites are $1.40 per person, cabins are $7.50 for two.

South New Brighton Park on Halsey St. in South New Brighton is 10km from the Square, ph. 889-844. There are no cabins, tent sites are $2.25 for two. Take a New Brighton or South Brighton bus. The **Rawhiti Domain** on Shaw Ave. in New Brighton is 9km from the Square, ph. 887-408. It's near the beach and a New Brighton bus will get you there. Again, no cabins, tent sites are $2.25 for two. And finally, the **Aranui Holiday Camp** is at 121 Shortland St., ph. 888-703, take a New Brighton bus. Tent sites are $1.20 per person, cabins from $5 for two.

The bed and breakfast situation is really good in Christchurch, too. We found five for $10 or less. **Aarangi Guest House**, 15 Riccarton Rd., ph. 43-584, $8.50. **Ambassadors**, 19 Manchester St., ph. 67-808, $10. **Hotel Melville**, 49 Gloucester St., ph. 798-956, $9. **Windsor Private Hotel**, 52 Armagh St., ph. 61-502, $10. **Wolseley Lodge**, 107 Papanui Rd., ph. 556-202, $10.

FOOD   The **Vacation Hotel**, 760 Colombo St., has a smorgasbord luncheon daily from 12 to 2 for $5. It includes a terrific array of food, is a really good value if you're one of those people who can stock up on lunch and skip dinner. At the other end of the dollar sign — the **Gaslight Tavern**, one block south of the Square on Worcester St., still has a $1 lunch. You get meat, potatoes, veges, and bread and butter — and it's really good!

   Leonardo da Vinci's at 129 Manchester St. has fantastic pizzas at reasonable prices. And at the **Number 17 Coffee House** in Chancery Arcade the specialties are pancakes and exotic coffees. **Barnaby John's**, also in the Chancery Arcade has all sorts of inexpensive food.

   The **Dominion Hotel** has bistro lunches Monday through Saturday, and down the street in New Regent St., the **Sandwich Factory** has delicious wholemeal sandwiches for about a dollar.

   If you're willing to pay a little more try **The Farmyard** on Montreal St. & Oxford Tce. for good natural foods. **Brita's Steak and Omelette House** in the Gloucester St. Arcade and **The Coachman** in the Chancery Arcade have reasonably priced (not cheap) steaks.

ENTERTAINMENT   Christchurch is another university town, so there's usually something going on. For a quiet evening you might try the **Victorian Coffee Gallery** at Montreal St. & Oxford Tce., or if you feel like "getting down" try **Adam's Apple**, a licensed nightclub on Lichfield St. — open Wednesday through Saturday, 9 p.m. to 3 a.m. (about $3 cover).

On the Road to Picton

In Amberly, the **Country Cake Kitchen** has fantastic homemade pies and pasties. It's worth a stop.

Kaikoura, 191km north of Christchurch, is a good place to spend a night (or more). There's a youth hostel, motor camp, and some B&Bs. The main attraction of the area, besides the beautiful scenery and the excellent surf fishing, is the **seal colony** on the tip of the peninsula. You can walk quite near the seals at low tide, but try not to bother them and **never** cut off their exit to the sea.

NOTES

NOTES

NOTES

NOTES

NOTES